Christian
Education
for
Liberation

Christian Education for Liberation

and Other Upsetting Ideas

J.C. Wynn

Nashville • Abingdon

Christian Education for Liberation

Copyright © 1977 by Abingdon

Library of Congress Cataloging in Publication Data

WYNN, JOHN CHARLES, 1920-
  Christian education for liberation and other
upsetting ideas.
  Bibliography; p.
  Includes index.
  1. Christian education. I. Title.
BV1471.2.W96   268   76-57926

ISBN 0-687-07100-3

Scripture quotations are from the Revised Standard Version Common
Bible, copyrighted © 1973.

Chapters 5 and 6 are reprinted from Vol. LIV, No. 5 and Vol. LX, No. 2
of *Religious Education* by permission of the publisher, The Religious
Education Association, 409 Prospect St., New Haven, Conn. 06510.

MANUFACTURED BY THE PARTHENON PRESS AT
NASHVILLE, TENNESSEE, UNITED STATES OF AMERICA

TO MY
FATHER
Once a Sunday church
school teacher in classes
for young men at the
First Presbyterian Church
Johnstown, Pennsylvania

Contents

Preface

Saints and sinners both become the way they are through education. To understand how the educational ministry of the churches influences persons toward commitment and action, even by means of rather upsetting programs, is the objective of this book. Some of these contents are unconventional, some conventional; but all the chapters that follow have come out of classroom teaching in the consortium of theological seminaries at Rochester, New York: Colgate Rochester Divinity School/Bexley Hall/ Crozer Theological Seminary. It is a classroom that has seated young theological students, lay persons from local parishes, and clergy returning for their continued education, sometimes simultaneously. They have labored together with me over these questions, and we have come to see that these are the very questions raised today by people in the parish churches.

I understand Christian education to be the church's enterprise in teaching persons about God in Christ and his invitation to join in his mission of reconciliation. There are scores of other definitions of Christian education; I have collected a number of them myself, and know that we who write about this topic present divergent views of what Christian education is. In fact, the confusion of our time, along with the crisis of the churches and the uncertainty of not a few theologians, seems to have spawned still more definitions, each uncongenial with the preceding. Be that as it may, the attempt of this book is to answer a number of the frequently asked questions about education in the churches and to do so within the interpretation of Christian education cited above.

This synthesis of educational theory and information,

much of which is the common corpus of divinity school classrooms, is in six parts. The first chapter, "Memories of an Underground Seminary of Sorts," reviews a struggle with heretofore resistant theological students who became suddenly motivated to learn about Christian education, and a few of the lessons we covered. Chapter 2, "Reluctant Saints and the Mystique of Teaching," continues one part of that theme, namely, resistance to learning, but this time in the setting of the church where a clear idea of the teaching-learning transaction is essential. The currently fashionable topic of theology of liberation gets its deserved attention in chapter 3, the title essay of this volume, but with emphasis upon the educational implications of that theological material and its impact upon parish churches as "Education for Liberation and Other Upsetting Ideas." It is the vast and newly rediscovered subject of moral education that is examined in "Problems in Teaching People to Behave: Clarifying Some Values," the fourth chapter. If "The Real Impossibility of Christian Education" sounds as if the book should not have been written, please read on; for this fifth chapter deals with the problems of communication in our church teaching. I have long been fascinated by the hidden hope in the doctrine of eschatology and why this topic has become so scarce in church education; that is the concern of chapter 6, "Why the Conspiracy of Silence About Eschatology in Church Education?"

I take satisfaction in acknowledging the helpful influence upon my life and work of several admired authorities in the fields of education and of psychology, some of them my teachers of old, some of them colleagues, all of them friends. They are Luther Allen Weigel and Paul H. Vieth, who were my professors at Yale University Divinity School many years ago; C. Ellis Nelson and Phillip Phenix, who taught me at Union Theological Seminary and Columbia University Teachers College somewhat later; Paul Calvin Payne, whose leadership in Christian education has placed many of us in his debt; and three intimate colleagues over the years: Roy W. Fairchild, my occasional coauthor and a professor at the Graduate Theological Union in Berkeley; James B. Ashbrook, my fellow professor in Colgate Rochester/Bexley/Crozer; and Charles F. Melchert, my colleague and sometime team teacher over too brief a time in Rochester, and now on the faculty of the Presbyterian School of Christian Education. Of course, none of these men is to be charged with the opinions, errors, or shortcomings of this book; with some of the pages that follow, in fact, each might take exception. But I, like Tennyson's Ulysses, am part of all that I have met; and I am grateful to these scholars for much that I have learned.

To Randolph Crump Miller, the scholarly editor of the journal *Religious Education,* I am grateful for permission to reprint (now somewhat altered) articles that have appeared in past issues; these are incorporated here as chapters 5 and 6. Hazel P. Spaven has once again typed and helped edit my scrambled copy, a most appreciated favor; and Ellen J. Bulmore has graciously completed the final typing.

Roland Bainton once recorded the statistics of a Sunday school in New Haven *circa* 1827. At that time the record cited, ''There are 27 male and 35 female teachers all of whom are hopefully pious.'' Whether much can be said for the piety of these essays I dare not guess; but they are at least, I hope, useful.

J. C. WYNN

Memories of an Underground Seminary of Sorts

*The vitality of religion is shown
by the way in which the religious spirit has
survived the ordeal of religious education.*

Alfred North Whitehead

For some years I was guilty of operating an underground seminary of sorts—and right within the divinity school, where I'm employed to teach respectable, above-board courses. It all came about because of the reluctance of some students to register in time for courses in the educational ministries. A certain hard core of divinity students would rather have been caught in a Playboy Club than in a course in church education. Much rather, in fact.

They eschewed any education about education, nicknaming such courses Scissors and Paste 102, or Mickey Mouse classes. Not the ones to waste time in enterprises that deal with teaching, curricula, or developmental education, they made it clear they had Better Things To Do. Then along about February or March of their senior year, they would enter their first serious interviews for church positions and find that the most promising openings available to them were staff placements where they would be expected to specialize in educational ministry.

Too late now to enroll for the scorned courses but eager for the church positions that demand knowledge and techniques in church education, they arrived with lists of questions that could form a veritable syllabus:

How can I administer a church school?
What's the best curriculum publication?

12

Who knows anything about training teachers?
Name three good books on Christian education.
Where can I find material for a church membership
or confirmation class?
Give me some pointers to get started and keep one week
ahead of the pack till I can get acquainted with the job.

Do you notice how they still envisioned the task as
gimmicks, as manipulation, as Mickey Mouse? Programs,
publications, panaceas! And to be fair, why not? The
churches they hoped to land in often see the challenge just
that way—scissors and paste, filling expectations of yore
that, too often, were the members' previous Sunday church
school experiences. And they, all too readily, have been
willing to recapitulate it for their ministry also.

"O tempore, o mores," as Cicero, or someone who
spoke Latin, must have said. The challenge has driven us
together to organize sessions on where to find the resources
(printed, audio-visual—and, most of all, personal, external
and internal), how to work with the limitations of their
people, how to apply some of the knowledge they already
had stored away in undusted notebooks—about Scripture,
about personality development, about self-understanding,
about church tradition, about how to think theologically,
about God-talk, about the relation to contemporary social
change, and all those problems about which they had
written 3,000-word term papers, answered exam questions,
and stayed up late to cram, however briefly, into their tired
minds.

Under these circumstances the time is ripe for applied
Christianity, for practical theology, for bridging the gap
between the theoretical and the operational. We had reached

the teachable moment of readiness. If we were wise we would use it with something better than slogans, with directions toward programs a cut above gimmickery, with increased knowledge on how to communicate the meaning of faith revealed to us by God in Christ. This would be not simply a short course on how to appear expert enough to fool the committee into hiring them, or how to hang on to the job while learning enough to keep going. There is more to the task of church education than that.

Sunday Church School as Cinderella

Our problem is further exacerbated by the evidence that church education is in untidy disarray. Long the poor stepsister of the parish church, church education is a Cinderella who has worked away in the drudgery of Sunday church school and almost never had a ball.

The educational task of the church all too often has been confined to that venerable and fatigued institution, the Sunday church school. Experts in Christian education for years have decried the ineffectual, indeed often counter-productive, aspects of the poor old Sunday school; but it lives on as if it possessed the real secret of longevity. And those who have tried to kill it off in some ill-advised euthanasia program can only echo Macbeth's plaint after knifing Duncan: "Who would have thought the old man had . . . so much blood in him?"

I had my own comeuppance some twenty years ago in writing an article for *The Christian Century* in which I tolled the bell for a decent burial and kind obituary for the Sunday church school. My article never laid a glove on the institution; it only succeeded in angering some people in the

Presbyterian Board of Christian Education, which, at the time, was paying my salary.

We do well to ponder the mystery of why the Sunday church school persists despite all its ills and injuries, despite all that we dislike and disrespect in it. The clues stand out all around us: (1) The Sunday church school has traditionally served as a feeder for the membership of the church institution. In an insidious chicken-and-egg syndrome—when the Sunday church school declines, so does the church body, and we do well not to destroy the despicable thing until we secure enough other evangelistic vehicles that match its power. (2) The Sunday church school has been, indeed remains, a source of vitality for the whole church, socializing the young and promising a new generation of would-be saints. (3) The Sunday church school has a form and a function that have been ingrained into our system and ritual so that, whatever we say against this amateur bureaucracy, we'd better not sacrifice it until we are certain we won't lose more assets than liabilities therein.

Our task is to stare down these awkward educational embarrassments eyeball to eyeball. You are invited to the contest.

In so doing, we are obliged to adopt the bridge engineer's strategy: we continue to use the old bridge while building the new. Just as many a parish now offers two distinct types of divine worship—both the old, old traditional liturgy, with its psalms and robes, and the new, contemporary service, with its popcorn, balloons, and guitars—so we can abide the unsinkable Sunday church school while working on new educational experiments.

But the Sunday church school's prognosis is grim, and we must keep working at new forms to take over the educational mission of the church. The Sunday church school had its zenith in the nineteenth century, when most of our denominations were swept by evangelical revivalism. Child prodigy of that grand sweep of evangelism, the Sunday church school made a powerful impact and grew mightily. Massive Sunday school parades, unbelievable now to us, were held in American cities on Rally Day; captains of industry paid public homage to their Sunday school teachers; missionaries were inspired and financed by these classes; and these bands of thrilled Christians marched into the bright light of God's sunshine as if there would be no tomorrow. But their tomorrow became our today. And the few settings in which the Sunday church schools now flourish are to be found chiefly in conservative, evangelical, or Pentecostal denominations, whose style is akin to that of nineteenth-century revivalism. The major denominations will not again see the Sunday church school in the glory of preeminence.

The history of how we arrived at this point is of interest, at least to Christian educators. That religious enthusiasm bore up well into the present century. Gradually it became intermixed with the new progressive education, and the effect upon Protestant churches was profound. By the 1930s, Christian liberalism, linked with such names as Edgar Sheffield Brightman, Shirley Jackson Case, and Douglas Clyde Macintosh, infiltrated our major denominations. Personalism, ethical humanism, theology as an empirical science, and an uncritical idealism were some marks of this liberal era. We lived in the assumption that the ethics of Jesus could be caught rather than taught, that children and youth would naturally absorb their faith somehow from adults who had all too little of it! The

16

process by which the faith was handed down (note that condescending figure of speech) was then known as *religious education*.

But a famous bomb had fallen on the playground of the theologians: Karl Barth's theology exploded not only his own early liberalism but nearly everyone else's too. The powerful impact of continental theology leaped the Atlantic and hit America in the 1940s and 50s. It was a time of rapid church growth, of a building boom in which new church architecture kept pace with boxy housing in the suburbs. National church agencies, heady with widespread support and loyalty, all developed new curriculum publications in investments of millions. A vast recruitment and training program was instituted for Sunday school teachers to inculcate the many children from the baby boom during this seemingly endless growth. And the practitioners of my craft, atuned to the times of neo-orthodoxy, changed the name of their work from *religious education* to *Christian education* to show they were with it, meanwhile reading the Bs of Barth, Brunner, Bonhoeffer, Bultmann—but not Billy! (See William Franklin Graham, *America's Hour of Decision.*)

It couldn't last, and it didn't. Uneasy questions about unnerving new developments in church giving and membership growth began to emerge as we entered the sixties. Existentialists meanwhile were teaching us something about our own participation in faith, casting some shadow upon revelation theology in our neo-orthodox interpretation. A wholly new wave of secularism burst loose. God was dead. Civil rights marches became a new liturgy. Ecumenism leveled barriers and also some convictions. Social activism was teaching the faithful far more than any classes in dogma. The names of Paul Tillich, William Hamilton, and John XXIII appeared in church school quarterlies. Sunday church attendance declined. Young people dropped out. Our young adults who had been tutored through the forties and fifties turned out now to have very unimpressive biblical faith. They seemed unable fully to understand the mission of the church in our world. They could seldom grasp what their national denominational leaders were about as they preached about a newly emerging Christian social consciousness. The Sunday church school had faltered. Forced to see our task in larger terms, we changed our name again; now we were in *church education*.

With the uncertain seventies we became accustomed to specialized theologies: black theology, charismatic Pentecostalism, theology of hope, liberation theology, the new evangelism. But the comfort of an old party line, such as neo-orthodoxy, was gone. And to complicate it all, the psychologists (Jean Piaget, Jerome Bruner, Lawrence Kohlberg, B. F. Skinner, *et al.*) were throwing conflicting challenges at all educators. The influence of church educators is dwindling; the work is at times demoralized and jobs in the profession are scarce. We church educators have not even found a new name for ourselves this decade!

A crisis is upon us. We see it in the macrocosm as the institutional churches stumble in confusion. We see it in the microcosm as individual ministers struggle and search for meaning in their work, and guidance in their education. The denominations lack authority just now; our leaders lack credibility. And the very term *Sunday school stuff* summons up visions of the innocuous and the irrelevant. It is an epithet of opprobrium on a level with *Boy Scout troop*. Churches show their loss of nerve in myriad ways,

Currently, there is too much retreat into the parochial, the petty, the safe and narrow. And this teaches a powerful, unintended lesson that probably exceeds the influence of our curriculum efforts. We begin to ask the wrong questions—queries about method (scissors and paste) instead of about mission. We lose touch with our purpose. As church-in-the-world we must also keep in touch with our tradition. Yet we must also avoid traditionalism, the petty concern with long gone trivia of the past whose litanies no longer awaken any responses. Our failures in church education have been close to our failures in maintaining a vital faith and mission, not our problems of method or Mickey Mouse gimmickery.

Some Admonitions

Church education always reflects, like a mirror, the image of the body ecclesiastic itself. Seldom do we see a strong church with weak education or, obversely, a weak church whose educational program is very good. Indeed, if current tendencies persist without amelioration, future generations will face dark ages in which they could be denied an understanding of Christian faith and order. Our institutional church is always just about one to two generations from extinction. The church, therefore, *must* teach or die out.

Perhaps we can clear our vision sufficiently and describe our dream courageously enough to steer through current crises. If that is to be, then we will have to acknowledge some basic truths.

First, the church is not simply an institution useful for a community, like a bank or the town dump, but a fellowship in Jesus Christ, who founded it. The Christian church exists wherever his faith is taught and carried into action.

19

Second, church doctrine determines the quality of its education; and if we are unsure of our doctrine, then we blow our educational trumpet with embarrassing uncertainty. Church education remains dependent upon the church's theology.

Third, whether we recognize it or not, the entire church has some educational influence: surely the preacher in the pulpit, but also the usher on the side aisle, the altos in the choir, the sexton by the kitchen door. And what these people teach willy-nilly may exceed any learning from the curriculum that some commission had planned.

Fourth, the church has had her most famous educational successes when she carried out her mission, confirming that God has acted in Christ, liberating humankind, conquering sin and death.

Fifth, we shall get nowhere if we continue to give low priority to commitment and discipline, to inculcating the faith, and to an educational enterprise of integrity. Only low-grade education can result.

What respectable leads might then be shown to a young minister about to enter a parish church where he or she is expected to be a pastoral educator?

The young minister about to enter a parish ministry as a pastoral educator will need more than how-to manuals and a closet full of curriculum supplies. In the direct, second-person address I have used in the theological seminary classroom, I would say there are four basic principles for you to note.

First, you need to know that you cannot wait until all the church's problems are solved and tidied up before taking up your task, nor can you allow these difficulties to deter you from the daily struggle of ministerial work. None of us can wait until these vicissitudes of faith and order are past before we continue our ministry of education.

Second, you are not alone anyway. There is a priesthood of believers out there, a lay ministry you will join. Do locate and cooperate with the commission on church education in the parish. Thus you will share ideas and decisions, responsibility and friendship, credit and blame.

Third, don't use your influence before you have any. Allow enough time for mutual trust to develop before introducing your own startling innovations. Thereafter you will find yourself revising even some of your most brilliant ideas.

The fourth is like unto it: start where your church people are before pressing them on to new advances. A new parson enters into congregational life that largely influences the effectiveness and quality of its education. You need not alienate the slow, faithful members; they just might possess some local folk wisdom that is not apparent to you at first. Find your way into the system before you attempt anything radical, *i.e.,* disturb their roots. In an aphorism of one of my friends, "If the pewholders appear to be getting along somehow, for God's sake leave them alone!" (That is more a prayer than blasphemy.)

Yet there are several practical, active measures any minister can take early in this educational ministry. You can pick up a teaching task yourself, *e.g.,* a children's division on Wednesday afternoon after school (making sure that you have some parent helpers) or a unit in church-officer training. The people will see you as one who is teacher. You could do worse than that; we have, in fact, a New Testament precedent.

You can also multiply your loaves by teaching teachers.

Aid those already in the work and the new recruits who are soon to begin, by offering courses in Bible, in theological doctrine, in church history. These are enrichment courses for them and for you too.

Moreover, make friends with community educators who can lead you to useful resources: local experts, film libraries, secular materials in magazines or TV programs, ecumenical opportunities, and many more. There are astonishing aids scattered all about.

But do not neglect to learn early what publications your denomination offers; these ought to supply the best "fit" for your church. However, don't stop there. You can cheerfully mix and match a variety of materials for the profit of your people. This, I realize, is arguable; and I am opinionated on the point, but from experience. You can draw intelligently from Lutheran, Catholic, and humanistic psychology sources with profit.

Often the clergy tend to forget that the teaching task of the church is its mission, its very apostolate. Yet when they are convinced of that truth, it will alter profoundly their attitude as well as their work in educational ministry. It is then that they begin to devote significant time and effort to study and teaching, a discipline that too many clergy have neglected to their own great loss. Now, more than ever before, this obligation is crucial to the waning health of a parish. The problem has been that serious study is so easy to skip that many clergy discontinue it.

The time will come, however, when such a scholarly pastor will understand his or her ministry as a whole, without separating out the educational role as if it were some highly advertised but superfluous additive. This will help keep alive the memory that the way we conduct our very relationships is also a teaching function. It is not only in a classroom that we educate; our resolutions of official board arguments about budget likewise teach someone something. The manner in which we administer church business cannot escape educational implications. There is simply no way of avoiding the educational aspects of ministerial life, whether we are instructing, counseling, or just negotiating our differences.

In addition, the minister's educational work is going to be more effective if educational objectives are clear. Unless both clergy and parishioners understand what the goals are for a certain course, and how these work into church policy, the teaching cannot be effectively communicated; and it will frustrate and confuse. Many a parish has never sorted out the objectives to discover whether they teach church school pupils in order to placate certain prominent adults or in order to aid the pupils to think theologically on their own.

That there is much more involved than materials and methods, techniques of teaching, and audio-visual aids in church education becomes cogent to the reluctant and the recalcitrant theologues who had planned to avoid the subject and who had slandered it with slogans and epithets. The centrality of education in parish life begins to become more and more evident, as well as the minister's need to become more proficient in it.

In recent years theological students have been returning to educational courses in seminaries all across the nation, and I no longer conduct my underground seminary. In common with clergy everywhere, they now are beginning to see the importance of education to church life and the necessity to engage themselves as teachers. For that, we, with the Apostle, can "thank God and take courage."

Reluctant Saints and the Mystique of Teaching

I believe that teaching is an art not a science.
It seems to me very dangerous to apply the aims and
methods of science to human beings as individuals. . . .
Teaching involves emotions, which cannot be system-
atically appraised and employed, and human values,
which are quite outside the grasp of science. . . .
Teaching is not like inducing a chemical reaction:
it is much more like painting a picture or making a
piece of music, or on a lower level like planting a
garden or writing a friendly letter. You must throw
your heart into it, you must realize that it cannot
all be done by formulas, or you will spoil your work,
and your pupils, and yourself.

Gilbert Highet

In an astonishing and controversial statement, Jerome S. Bruner has contended that the foundations of any subject may be taught to anybody at any age in some form. To that contention many an educator's response has been, "Well, maybe." The bravado of such a claim sweeps aside the theories of developmental psychology that a person must have reached an appropriate maturity before he can grasp certain ideas. It also ignores that favorite corollary of educators, the readiness theory, which would be cited to explain why a child is not yet at the "teaching moment" to learn calculus or art history or dogmatic theology. But its chief fault, as I see it, is that such a courageous statement fails to take fully into account the pupil's resistance to being taught.

Pedagogical resistance is an endemic problem among the

churches. Negative reaction to Christian education is so widespread that wherever ministers and church teachers gather for workshops and conferences, they flock to discussions about how to motivate the learner. This problem is a brutal one in ecclesiastical circles, although we certainly also share it with public schools, adult education programs, and even graduate schools. It will be helpful to review, then, what makes for learning resistance, what makes for learning motivation, and how the teaching-learning transaction can work for us.

Learning Resistance

The church educator is expected to teach those who are "called to be saints," as Paul dubs them (Romans 1:7). Very often, however, the saints respond with massive reluctance to being taught, a challenge we have noted that we have in common with other institutions. That reluctance pops up in enrollment for courses, in attendance at sessions, in attention during sessions, and a myriad of ingenious and disingenuous ways.

It is not appropriate, however, for us simply to deplore their recalcitrance—those old and young, rich and poor, male and female who resist our attempts to enlighten them. They may, as we see below, have justifiable reasons. In any case, our assignment is to face the challenge rather than simply complain about it. They have their reluctance, but we have our work in education. These two conflict.

What inspires (if that is the word) such resistance to learning? First, a paucity of any readiness for education to begin with; some have come to church for other reasons than to receive a Christian education, and its presence is for them tantamount to an intrusion. It is a problem that goes back many centuries. Even in A.D. 350, Cyril of Jerusalem was addressing the catechumens of his diocese regarding their lack of motivation:

> Perhaps you had a different reason for coming. For it is quite what might happen, that a man should be wanting to advance his suit with a Christian woman, and to that end has come here. And there is the like possibility the other way round. Or often it may be a slave that wanted to please his master, or a person that comes for the sake of his friend. I accept this as bait for the hook, and I welcome you as one who shall be saved, by a good hope, in spite of having come with an unsound intention. It may well be that you did not know . . . what sort of a net is taking you. And now you are inside the ecclesiastical fishnets. Let yourself be taken, do not make off, for Jesus is angling for you. . . .

Second, they come in from a secularized society whose values neither coincide nor harmonize with the church's ideals on a great many points. In their eyes the church has suffered a devaluation of influence, and theology is of little importance. In this they are partially correct. The questions they are asking do not appear to them to have theological implications. What is more, theology is rarely credited with having any truths to meet their queries. They little know nor long remember that the church's thinkers have historically constructed their theology out of grappling with secular problems. They only conclude that little can be gained by trying to learn from such an institution as the church.

Third, they may realize as fully as we that Christianity, in the words of Abbé Michonneau, "has become static and no longer conflicts with persons' lives." Instead of a dynamic faith or a relevant belief system, they confront a defensive

26

religion, clutching its traditions and hopes, its rites and reputation, its assets and relics. All that hardly prepares a climate for learning.

Fourth, the church has probably been unwise, we now believe, so long to have retained the public school model as a paradigm of educational organization. It is a model that has hot been very useful to the church for some decades. It is not even viable for public education any longer, according to Ivan Illich and a host of critics who have gone about the campaign of "deschooling society." Our tendency has been not only to adopt the model of the public school, but also to reproduce many of its worst mistakes complete with classes, departments, and graduations, to the end that when we get children or adults into classes they are subjected to "an information overload" (the term is Marshall McLuhan's). And a bored pupil promptly joins the resistance movement in education; actively or passively she or he will hold out against effective learning and thwart the efforts of the best laid curriculum plans.

Fifth—and this could be the very nadir of their difficulties—they might just suspect what psychological tests (*e.g.*, those of Milton Rokeach) find: that people who get religion often turn out to be more bigoted, less humanitarian, and less stable in some respects than the unchurched! Who needs that?

Our church educators find this all very disconcerting. They have their teaching objectives (to pick up their own lingo) to introduce persons into the worship habits and cultural expectations of their denomination, to promote understanding of their history, to help them know their Scriptures, to open the way to a deeper understanding of the saving knowledge of God. There is so much to learn! It is frustrating that people avoid it.

To these five problems could be added five times five more. The causes of educational resistance are actually counted in the dozens under such headings as Unconscious Defenses, Conflicts, Competitive Needs, Personal Prejudices, and so on.

But Learning Comes Naturally

Moreover, learning is one of the essential characteristics of human beings. Humans are natural learners; and you cannot prevent them from learning, beginning with Day One in their lives. Left to themselves they will observe, reason, adopt, adapt, devise, revise, imitate, accommodate, appropriate, innovate, contemplate, associate, assimilate, investigate, memorize, theorize, criticize, realize, intellectualize, study, figure, puzzle, ponder, peruse, understand, grasp, and know! If they are left to themselves, I said. That is, in their natural state they are natural learners.

Why, then, should we ever intervene to program their learning or interfere with their growing knowledge? Because under circumstances of uninterrupted unconscious learning they tend to repeat over and over the learnings of others, fall into *their* pitfalls, and remake *their* same old mistakes. Thus through repeated trial and error, then trial and success, they return full circle to the place they began and fail to recognize it. Like their ancestors, they would wander around in the desert for forty years, worship at the shrines of false gods, or deny their Lord and crucify him anew.

We show an odd tendency to reinvent the wheel. We tend

to repeat the history of the past because we fail to understand it. We waste our efforts and our substance in unnecessary relearning. We are not better than our fathers.

The major system we have that can break into that profitless cycle of reliving and rehearsing the same lessons by blind chance and by vain repetition is to introduce *planned learning*. That is a process called *education*.

Education makes it possible to stand on the shoulders of our forebears and to see farther than they saw, to utilize the insights of the past and to make new gains based on the gains of our ancestors, to grasp in ten minutes what it has taken the race centuries to understand.

Education enables us to transmit the tradition, reproduce the ritual, and continue the culture. A mutual, interpersonal meeting, it facilitates the process whereby the old teach the young about their heritage. But it also opens the way for youth to induct their elders into new occasions and new duties, to introduce the future era, to teach the modern ways. It is a two-way traffic of mutual edification. When it works well, it can be a beautiful interaction; when it fails, it can lead to disaster.

The Teaching-Learning Transaction

That mutual, interpersonal meeting in education is the teaching-learning transaction. It offers more promise than learning theories *per se* (that solid collection of overlapping explanations of how we catch on through association, assimilation, rewards and penalties, reinforcement, operant conditioning, and all the other slogans of educationists). It also offers more promise than what Jerome Bruner calls ''a theory of instruction,'' whereby we specify (1) the experiences meant to implant a predisposition to learning, (2) the ways in which a body of knowledge can be structured so that it can be grasped, (3) the most effective sequences in which to present material, and (4) the nature and pacing of rewards and/or penalties. There is learning theory, and there is instruction theory; but obviously one without the other stands alone in barren isolation.

It will be useful, therefore, for us to review a transactional analysis of the teacher-learner dyad; for the nexus that Nathaniel Cantor once named "the teaching-learning transaction" is a viable educational theory for anyone, but especially for us in Christian education with all of its theology of relationships.

Knowing something about the games people play, we realize the importance of defining the persons in any transaction and what personal baggage they bring into it. Here we have the learner who totes a very mixed bag of characteristics: his or her abilities and disabilities, needs and hopes, ignorance and information, resistance or openness, past experience, latent anxiety, lethargy, and natural desire to learn. Here also is the teacher who carries into this transaction his or her own anxieties, needs, experience, ignorance, and more or less openness; and in addition, his knowledge of the subject, skills in organizing that knowledge, awareness of relationships and how to repair them, some acceptance of the learner and of the learner's limitations. The learner and the teacher make up a human relationship with all its possibilities for good and ill. During their interaction they will change roles several times as the teacher learns from the student and becomes the taught instead of the pedagogue. That transaction between them moves both ways in their common understanding

Just as each brings some personal baggage into the transaction, each carries something away. If the educative process was real, they leave with fresh knowledge—and new ideas, reformed opinions, changed attitudes, and a meaningful interpersonal relationship bonded between them.

The social psychologists have researched for us some of the ways this process has evolved, and their research findings are enlightening for the teacher working with reluctant (yes, even saintly) learners. Edwin P. Hollander has compiled data from this research to show where teaching motivates learning and conquers resistance:

1. The *friendly* teacher makes a greater impact on learners and communicates more directly with them. Such a teacher actually likes students. This increases the influence of the teacher, motivates the learner, and aids the more profound changes of attitude. What is more, the positive expectation of the teacher that the learner is capable increases the rate at which the learner absorbs new knowledge.

2. Second, the teacher who encourages active *participation* in the learner brings about greater changes in learning than ever happens in the passive listening role. There is a label on that passive role—the "Jug-Mug Theory"—wherein the teacher thinks he is imparting knowledge to waiting minds as if pouring contents into open craniums. It is one of the ironies of theological seminary education that we are accused of not teaching our students how to teach and of fostering too many poor examples that later are repeated in a thousand parish churches. There is much to be said for lecturing—for example, it passes data on more rapidly than other methods; but it must be intermixed with other media that involve more active participation lest it

avoid the Jug-Mug fallacy. Active participation, on the other hand, places responsibility upon the pupil to select his or her own objectives and to program the necessary learning to meet these objectives. As no one else can effectively do this for the pupil, this step is essential; but it is ironical how often we seek to circumvent it. More class participation through group discussion, role-playing, simulations, case studies, and other methods in which the students make major investment begins to produce the change that all educators seek.

3. The teacher who involves the group in *mutual support* is going to see more gains in education than one who does not. Our research in social psychology implies that group support enables the learner to make greater change in attitudes and performance. Experiments have shown that both our thinking and action are more profoundly altered when our peers show us positive regard and that, conversely, an unfriendly peer group (and a hostile teacher too) can stagnate learning changes.

Behind such interpersonal relationships of teacher and learner are two basic theoretical assumptions. One is that this transaction is a dynamic, interactive process (there is nothing static and placid here) between them. The human interaction in education must be dynamic because there are few measurable gains from passive acceptance of knowledge. We must watch out for this because pupils are often adept at encouraging teachers to allow the more passive and less effective types of education and, as Leland Bradford notes, "by their satisfaction in being protected from important learning, reward teachers for ineffective teaching and thus perpetuate poor teaching."

The other assumption is that the objective of all education

is change and growth in the individual, and this is especially true in educating persons Christianly. We must realize that any cognition that does not require us to relate and reorganize our internal and external worlds cannot guarantee growth but becomes profitless education. We must keep remembering that nothing is taught until someone has learned. And no real learning has taken place until change is evident in the way we view and live our lives.

Mere Information Can Promote Resistance

Admit it we must: there are limits to the value of acquiring plain knowledge. We teach all about a subject instead of what the subject is all about. And that invites resistance.

What's so wrong with imparting information? After all, a teacher must know and even like the subject. We've all heard of the teacher who taught so near the edge of the subject that he frequently fell over the bluff. But Alfred North Whitehead reminds us in *The Aims of Education* that education is not a process of packing articles into a trunk and that knowledge does not keep any better than fish.

In any case, mere information accrual fosters occasional reluctance on the part of everyone except the pedant and the grind. Knowledge is a process and not a product, as Jerome Bruner notes. Knowledge must be usable, and it has to be internalized in order to be effective. Outside the learner, it tends to become compartmentalized. We all know more than we know that we know anyway, as Thornton Wilder wrote in his *Eighth Day;* and efficient learning demands that we draw out (that is, educe) that which we scarcely realize that we own.

Moreover, biblical knowledge, by itself, has long been an unconnected mass for most church people. Unless they can see themselves in the biblical narrative, the Bible remains to them that dust-covered, irrelevant book.

But if they can identify with the Bible's teachings, as Sören Kierkegaard did, they will iternalize their learning. Kierkegaard related how he read the parable of the good Samaritan. When he read of the priest who passed by the mugging victim, he responded, "I am like that priest." When he read of the Levite who looked on the beaten victim and kept going, he said, "I am like that Levite." But when he read of the Samaritan who stopped, aided the victim, carted him to an inn, left a deposit and a promissory note, he could only say, "I am *not* like that Samaritan."

God is so far beyond mere human understanding that theologians are ever and always at pains better to communicate the faith, but it is a work with its limitations because mere verbal teaching cannot accomplish it. God-talk alone is not sufficient, as everyone knows. Until the message is appropriated by the learner through a realized Presence, a fellowship with God, an experience of God in Christ, a mystical experience, a direct awareness—or something personal and individual—his or her internal world remains untouched and unchanged. Our learner may know about the faith but not possess faith for self, may memorize the data but not appropriate the meaning in life. That learner goes far to demonstrate the finitude of our educational programs.

Real education requires a dynamic transaction between a personable teacher of skill and knowledge with a ready learner who is open to constructive change in living. A tall order, that!

34

The Teacher as Interlocutor

More often than not, it is the teacher who must take the initiative in the educational process, even though learners bring their hopes and needs and even demands. Learners never come to us in shiny new *tabula rasa* style. They already have knowledge of thousands of items, and some of this is even relevant. They all know more than they know that they know. The teacher's work is to educe that knowledge, display it to its owner, test it, enrich it, add to it, and motivate the learners to handle and improve upon their knowledge.

It is for the teacher to guide the learner toward what Abraham Maslow used to call self-actualization. Boldly expropriated by the Christian teacher, this concept means that the learner begins to understand himself/herself as a child of God, to learn what is involved in being obedient to God in Christ, to reach self-actualization as a mature disciple.

True education is always a discovery trip. The learner gains the thrill of discovery for herself or himself of what is to be grasped. Significant understanding comes when the student sees that the subject material is personally usable. As Carl Rogers reminds us, really good education has to mean "I am discovering." This is the heuristic experience, so valuable to any person in self-affirmation; it is the thrill of seeing connections and the whole. It is what George B. Leonard named "education and ecstasy."

There are few thrills to equal the lure of working on your own educational goals. A colleague of mine tells students that when the time comes that they become so involved in library research that they forget to come out from the book stacks to go to dinner, then they are actually caught up in the thrill of learning.

Yet education is not an individualistic quest alone. The transaction necessitates a teacher. Meanwhile the teacher is at the job, introducing an important quantum of resources.

1. The teacher brings greater knowledge into the transaction. His or her objective is not just to tell the learners what this knowledge is (although it's easier, of course, to tell them than to open the doors for discovery). The teaching task is to lead the learner to do his or her own thinking, searching, appropriating.

Such a teacher must needs be well informed, must keep up studying, indeed keep abreast of more information than he or she ever uses. This reserve supply of learning is the mark of a conscientious instructor.

Whitehead once told an audience of educators that a teacher should show himself as an ignorant man in the act of thinking. Such a human approach is the mark of an honest scholar.

2. The effective teacher also utilizes effective methods she or he has found productive. These methods must be arranged in order, because it is only planned learning that can be truly educational. Mere techniques become so-called gimmicks if they are not planned and integrated with a curriculum. Some of the best methods, if thus integrated, include trans-generation classes, teaching clusters, and the planning of such rites as the service of divine worship. They boast such novelties as learning centers, videotape, individualized studies, and interviews.

3. The teacher necessarily brings along his or her own personality. Must of our best teaching is done by the use of

oneself. The experienced teacher knows the function of trust and influence. We read in *The Education of Henry Adams:* "A teacher affects eternity; he can never tell where his influence stops." Books on great teachers are invariably paeans. What they have in common is a picture of persons who give generously of themselves. Research demonstrates that the teacher's personality is a better predictor of pupil achievement than the materials or literature in the curriculum.

4. The teacher is a person of conviction. That affects the learning profoundly. Abraham Lincoln was right on target: "If you believe in great ideas," he said, "you may be able to get others to believe in them." Mary Ellen Chase echoed him with "no one can effectively communicate an idea in which he is not consumingly interested himself." Surely such observations apply to the Christian teacher's personal faith. A teacher ought not to hide convictions or shield beliefs. Let pupils see teachers unmasked and honest in their belief system and their own faith.

The objective of education, we have repeatedly noted, is change. So much the more is the objective of Christian education a profound change in personal life. Indeed, we aim toward a new being, a transformation of the person into a new creature in Christ. The process by which this significant change is brought about has historically been known as conversion. It is a goal toward which the Christian educator works.

Whenever we have assumed that it is our duty to teach persons *about* faith instead of helping them to claim faith for themselves, we have failed Christian education. We have only accomplished an intellectualizing that fails to touch life. But true faith is deeper than, and far beyond beliefs, rituals, customs, and dogma. Our best service on behalf of the faith of Christians is to perform conscientiously our part of the transaction in the dialogue between committed teacher and the learner, no matter how reluctant.

Education for Liberation and Other Upsetting Ideas

The theological community has had to take risks and to speak of revolution. The theologians live in a world wherein, as Robert McAfee Brown put it, people live who hold four aces and are not asking for a new deal. In that world of abundance, most are hungry; in that world of affluence, most are unsheltered; in that world of technological mastery, few live by promise or share hope; in that world of potency, few have freedom.

Martin E. Marty and Dean G. Peerman

Were it not for liberation theology and its insistent voice, we might go on for decades discussing our problems of church education in business-as-usual tones, ever inferring that manageable alterations can be adopted in orderly fashion by logical committees. But we now find the churches under heavy attack by sharp critics (*e.g.*, Berger, Hamilton, and Rokeach). We are told that unless we revolutionize our educational emphases, we may witness the finish of the institutional church. We are facing brutal challenges, and we are not ready.

Confronted with global problems, the church is compelled to face the issue of whether she will continue to tinker with revised methods or meet the more radical question of revolutionizing her entire structure and operation. Perhaps the ax is laid to the root of the tree (Matthew 3:10). Yet change is difficult, even painful, to many churches. They will study change all right—but in order to arrest it. Appealing to tradition as if the mere fact that it is old, and its roots historical, makes it holy, many persons maintain faith, hope, and determination that there will be no change. Theirs is a stance of traditional*ism*, really; and thus it will continue until Christians are courageous enough to explore the alternatives. That our church schools have actually no right to exist unless they are organized to change both persons and society is a startling idea that could never occur to most Christians without massive help. They might then come to understand that we must learn to change, but they would still be far from the revolutionary theologian Paulo Freire's striking claim that we must *change to learn*.

Finding ourselves among the peoples who are privileged to have plenty in a world of scarcity, North Americans are challenged by severe ethical and religious problems. Pained by the growing realization that our own wealth is costly to the world at large, we Christians, in particular, cannot ignore this situation. With population outracing food resources, with Third World peoples poignantly aware of their poverty and of our affluence, the problem still worsens. We Christians in the developed countries cannot willfully remain ignorant of the facts or careless about alleviation. It is a time for education for liberation.

Life on our planet is becoming dreadfully more difficult to maintain. Two-thirds of the world's people are hungry and undernourished. By the year 2000, world population is projected to double, and food scarcities will become acute. We in the United States of America, though only 6 percent of the world's population, control 80 percent of the globe's income. The gap between rich and poor is wide now, and it is expected to grow yet wider by this century's end. What is more, the poor are increasingly aware of their plight. Their need is matched by their anger, but not by our caring. Their realization that impoverishment in underdeveloped nations is reciprocally connected to conspicuous waste of natural resources in developed countries brings our world ever closer to global danger, highlighting the immoral greed of the haves and the pitiful plight of the have-nots. If theology is an attempt to understand problems of the world *sub specie aeternitatis,*—under the aspect of eternity—then ours is a question for theologians and church educators together.

A Theology of Liberation

Although its strident note sounds new, the current cry for liberation has roots (*i.e., radix* in Latin) that reach far back into biblical history. Israel's Lord was the God of deliverance, pledging to Moses: "I have seen the affliction of my people who are in Egypt, and have heard their cry because of their taskmasters . . . and I have come down to deliver them" (Exodus 3:7-8). This is the God who also calls upon his people to leave their former secure homes in order to plunge into new areas still unknown to them. He had inspired his prophet Isaiah to compose:

> The Spirit of the Lord God is upon me,
> because the Lord has anointed me to bring good
> tidings to the afflicted;
>   he has sent me to bind up the brokenhearted,
> to proclaim liberty to the captives,
>   and the opening of the prison to
>   those who are bound.
>   Isaiah 61:1

Thus, when Jesus repeated these lines of poetry at Nazareth, he was identifying himself as liberator (Luke 4:16-30).

Some scholars (*e.g.,* Alan Richardson) are at pains to demonstrate that Jesus was not a revolutionary, but it is undeniable that the law-and-order authorities of his time

41

found him so subversive that the political-religious establishment had him put to death. To this day humanity looks to his example for guidance in teaching and applying what Walter Rauschenbusch named the social gospel. Citing Jesus' example, Helder Camara and sixteen other Roman Catholic bishops of the Third World have published a statement that applies that gospel to their lands and their peoples.

> Jesus in fact took upon Himself all mankind to lead it to eternal life, for which the earthly preparation is social justice, first form of brotherly love. When Christ frees mankind from death by His resurrection, He leads all human freedoms to their eternal fulfilment.

Once there was an era in which bishops did not speak with such boldness for social justice and human freedom, at least not in the very nations where the privileged and the rich have oppressed the deprived and poor. But times are abruptly changing. The poor are more numerous. The wretched of the earth are more knowledgeable. The resources of our planet world are more limited. The time for action is already past, and Christian leaders are trying to catch up. A staff paper, ''Learning in Context,'' circulated by the World Council of Churches, picks up the theme:

> Powers that are enslaving men are indeed rampant everywhere in the world today—enslaving the poor as well as the rich, the oppressed as well as the oppressors, making men less than human, as Jesus Christ has shown what it is like to be human, and keeping men from knowing the freedom of the children of God, and from enjoying the abundant and eternal life Jesus Christ has come to offer. Christian ministry is serving as God's agent in combating such powers.

You may have noted in both the Catholic and the World Council statements that there is a canny mixture of revolutionary rhetoric and evangelical message. Each is concerned with eternal life; each looks to Jesus Christ for salvation. The theologians of liberation do not lose sight of this point. They know that freedom from oppression means to be released not only from domination by tyrants without but also from the power of sin from within. Liberation from the bondage of oppressors is incomplete unless humankind also experiences freedom from their own sinfulness. In fact, history has often demonstrated that breaking the yoke of oppression can lead only to new oppressions, now by those who have been liberated, as they turn their freedom to new advantage for themselves and imitate the despicable behaviors of those they had opposed.

Jesus's preaching about the kingdom of God, with all its eschatological inferences, is also picked up by the liberation theologians to illuminate the contrast between the Christian ideal and the awful reality. As Richard Shaull notes, the kingdom of God always stands over every social and political order, thus exposing dehumanizing events. By contrasting how different our life on earth is from the picture of God's realm with its peace and plenty, its brotherhood and hope, its love and faith, the kingdom of God presses us with a challenge. As J. M. Lochman points out, a theology of revolution compels us to see that "We are living between the aeons, and are therefore caught up in the eschatological movement of God's Kingdom."

The kingdom of God, indeed, bears down upon our very lives. To take seriously our biblical theology clearly compels us to become involved in the struggle for God's will about justice and humanity in our time. We, as

Christians, have obligations here and now. "It is not with the next world that we are concerned, but with this world," Dietrich Bonhoeffer assured us. "What is above the world is, in the Gospel, intended to exist *for* this world."

When we review our religious heritage with its thundering God who demands, "Let my people go," its Messiah who proclaims the kingdom to "set at liberty those who are oppressed," and its eschatological expectations of justice for all humanity, we are forced into the conviction that we must have a mission of liberation. As Rubem Alves has noted:

> The community of Israel understood that the liberating events were not simply something of the past. The meaning which it derives from the Exodus is projected over the whole cosmos, space, and time. The God of the Exodus, consequently, is a living God! He is the power which fills the whole of reality with the promise of liberation revealed in the Exodus.

Our biblical language does look to the past tradition; but it is the bearer of promise, and it points toward the future. We cannot avoid the inference that a divine contemporaneity involves us now. Truly, where the Spirit of God is, there is freedom (II Corinthians 3:17).

Theologians of Revolution

Some theologians, in fact, go considerably farther than researching the questions of how God is speaking to our time through the history of suffering peoples. They advocate revolution. George Celestin, for instance, a theologian at St. Edward's University, contends that the church can no longer be content to alleviate the sufferings of victims of injustice; the churches may also have to preach violence. With Karl Rahner and others, he regards a struggle for power as inevitable and believes that churches must engage in changing unjust structures as soon as possible. To such theologians of revolution, the Christian pacifist's total renunciation of power is seen as irresponsible. Some have turned aside from Martin Luther King Jr.'s nonviolent philosophy to admire instead Mao's armed force. They recall Bonhoeffer's agonized decision to participate in the plot against Hitler's life, and praise that decision for its ethical realism. Some (*e.g.*, Robert McAfee Brown) have taken Thomas Aquinas' theory of a just war and applied it to a possible new theory of a "just revolution."

Richard Shaull is one theologian who advocates revolutionary action. He demands of Christian church people that they eschew the prejudice that all change should be gradual within the present system. This system, he believes, is a form of enslavement, and those who turn their backs on it for a revolutionary commitment offer "a small sign of hope for the world." Shaull insists that our faith and our contemporary history shove us toward the threshold of a new order. Only in and through struggle for liberation can we move to a fuller, richer life for all peoples. Not unmindful of the scandal in political theology that he espouses, Shaull boldly defends revolution as a viable Christian measure: "We are called to live in the world as a pilgrim people and to possess what we have as though we had it not."

Frederick Herzog, in a *Christian Century* article, emphasizes how God himself is the liberator of the human masses, a truth evident ever since God entered our world in the person of Jesus of Nazareth. Championing the weak and the powerless, God at the hinge of history came through the

Incarnation to liberate the locked-out and to redeem the oppressed. He offers to all of us our freedom—not so much freedom *from* as freedom *for,* not a negative gift, but a positive one. Our God-given freedom is to be used, according to his will, for reconciliation and not simply for our own personal (and selfish) salvation. The divine purpose in such freedom is to be found in a difficult ministry: "Mangled bodies, oppression and torture, humiliation and wretchedness—all this Jesus of Nazareth identifies with in corporate freedom, making it his own and turning it into newness of life."

Freedom is a mockery if it be used only for ourselves. The current lifeboat ethics, patterned on *triage,* would suggest that we garner our scarce resources for the most promising populations of humanity (ourselves included, of course) because there would not be enough to go around, and then make enlightened decisions regarding those who would be eliminated. But it is clear to Herzog, and it is incumbent upon all Christians to see, that life support systems of food and supplies are collapsing already for the wretched of the earth and that, at the present rate of consumption, they will also be exhausted for even the most affluent someday. In a striking metaphor, he imagines all humankind in a ship where the lower classes are shut up in leaky compartments while the first-class passengers enjoy the first-class dining room, not yet hit by the leaks. Obviously all of us will go down with this ship unless we acknowledge our interdependence and repair the leaks where the helpless are now suffering. It is a point repeatedly made by Barbara Ward in her often impassioned and always clear writings about our immorally uneven distribution of goods in this unjust world.

EDUCATION FOR LIBERATION

The Christian theologian's task is to ask again and again how God is working in our contemporary history and to dare answers to that question. Today's theologians cannot avoid the message that God is speaking to us all through the sufferings of millions. Of his own compassion and interest there should be little doubt. God takes sides with the oppressed! "Has not God chosen those who are poor in the world?" (James 2:5) Such a grim reminder helps correct the inexcusable heresy that never quite dies out, namely, that the fat-cat wealthy classes must somehow have earned God's favor by their meritorious works, else why are they so rich?

For a comprehensive educational view of the theology of liberation, however, we must turn to Paulo Freire's *Pedagogy of the Oppressed*. Freire is a vivid, driven man, once an educator in Brazil until his exile, then a member of the Harvard faculty before he became consultant to the educational division for the World Council of Churches. In his writing he is equally at home in quoting Fidel Castro, Paul, Karl Marx, and Jesus. With Lenin he avers that without a revolutionary theory there can be no revolutionary movement. And he sets out to construct such a theory, as a Christian, to aid the oppressed. Certain that our ontological vocation is to be subjects who act on and transform our world, he believes that each of us is capable of moving to new possibilities of more abundant life. Indeed each of us is obligated to act positively for such change. To affirm that persons should be free and then do nothing tangible about it is scandalous. Thus he would move all of us middle-class, sedentary ideologues into action. Freire, the radical, insists that radicalism is always creative and that radicalism liberates humankind. But most of us, he charges, are caught

47

in a bind of actually wishing to slow down any change in society, indeed actually increasing our commitment to an unchanging social situation.

Freire is convinced that education has a role in bringing about change and liberation, but it cannot be the education-as-usual programs to which we are accustomed. They, in point of fact, are instruments of further oppression, tending to hold down the masses and make them apathetic about ever achieving a decent chance. For Freire, education is never a neutral process. It either functions to facilitate conformity to the present system or else it becomes "the practice of freedom." Given today's explosive conditions of oppressed peoples in ethnic groups, in the Third World, and in our ghetto slums, inevitable conflict must be the result of either educational choice.

His book is for radicals; he hopes to arouse them to action. Vehement against the heresy that somehow the lot of the oppressed must be God's will, he inveighs against this "distorted view of God" and reminds the downtrodden of their God-intended rights. When the oppressed arise in revolution, it will eventually be a boon even to the oppressors, he contends. The oppressed restore a lost humanity to the oppressors as they deprive them of their power any longer to dominate and to oppress. Thus in one revolution it is possible for the oppressed to free both themselves and their oppressors. Revolution thus has a humanizing effect! For any oppressed persons to hold power back in the hopes that the oppressor will respond with softness is a false generosity. True generosity is hard, but this fight will actually constitute an act of love opposing the lovelessness of the oppressor's own violence. The trouble is that the oppressed have a fear of freedom that makes them no wiser than the oppressor they oppose, and when they gain the upper hand they frequently act just as he did. The oppressed must be taught to reject this image, to seize freedom and to use it constructively. In any case they would be justified in the use of violence because the oppressors have been using society's violence on them for years.

Thus Paulo Freire's radical theology interprets the more abundant life promised in the kingdom as a value to which men and women are entitled and which should be seized now. His seminars and writings have met with predictable censure within the councils of the churches; but we would do well to heed his upsetting ideas, for he speaks out of his Third World upbringing and he forces into our ken one type of reality about which we dare not be ignorant.

Freire has organized a system for teaching literacy by recruiting the newly taught and training them for participation in adult education among their own peoples. Convinced that privileged middle-class teachers (to him they are part of the oppressing forces whether they are conscious of it or not) cannot effectively instruct the wretched of the earth, he conceives of education as a subversive force. Educational projects must be organized and executed by the oppressed themselves, he believes. Oppressors can never be the educators in these situations; it is a contradiction of terms to suppose they would champion and implement a truly liberating education.

Through his work in jungle villages and urban slums, Freire, with his cohort, has labored hard to instill confidence in beaten peoples. His pupils will not at first take any initiative in their learning, but his methods compel them to. They tend to defer to any teaching authority, unaware that they themselves already have knowledge but have not yet organized it. They are frustrated and prone to violence in response to a violent society. With training they begin to understand that the exercise of power also includes other methods of persuasion. Freire's education for literacy includes much more than helping adults to learn to read and write; his system helps them to *see*. It is a model from which we also can learn.

For men and women to be illiterate in a reading world is to be visually handicapped. The handicap of illiteracy not only limits one in handling literature, but it also extends into relationships, politics, competence for employment, and self-esteem. Mass illiteracy (and indeed the functional illiteracy so widespread in our own nation) confirms people in their ignorance, their fatalism, and their helplessness before exploitation. It leads to dehumanization.

Yet ordinary, traditional education does not always correct the problem. Schooling, in fact, as Ivan Illich has suggested, serves often to alienate persons—bright from dull, persistent from drop-outs, graduates from the undergraduates, the educated from the unlearned. Education, by its very presence in a hamlet, can have an alienating effect or a reconciling effect. It can lift persons into new understanding and confidence; it can also abet the process of dehumanization. Education in our missions has been used, often unwittingly, to try to turn Africans into white Europeans, black Americans into Anglo-Saxon middleclass society, Orientals into Western Protestants. The failures of such misguided education can be seen on every side. Only a tiny minority of the oppressed who begin schooling ever graduate. Those who do, often find that their education has equipped them neither for a vocation that will support them nor for a life of harmony among their own people. Thus alienated both from gainful employment and from meaningful relationship, some become worse off with their diplomas than with their original ignorance. Not all missionary education, not all schooling can be tarred with this description; but enough reflects such failure that we must heed the lessons that Paulo Freire and his liberating educators would teach us about dehumanization.

We begin to see that a theology of liberation is only a speculative idea in the minds of some, but an explosive mixture in the praxis of others. We must be sophisticated enough to recall that radical actions begin first in the minds of theoreticians. It was not Einstein who dropped the A-bomb on Hiroshima, but it was his theory that made it possible. It was not Karl Marx who murdered the Kulaks—that was Stalin; but Marx's writings inspired the Soviet state. It is not Jürgen Moltmann who teaches the wretched to take up violence; but he works out the hermeneutics of "the living documents, institutions, and events in historical expressions of life *within their political context*" (my italics). And he it is who sees that the social revolution against unjust circumstances is "the immanent reverse side of the transcendent resurrection hope."

Theologies of liberation are upsetting to thoughtful persons precisely because they do affect our educational programs (secular and sacred) and can lead to action. That Christian action against oppression is mandatory is not doubted. The question is whether today's Christians can move soon enough with wise and compassionate programs.

The Church Cannot Keep Still

What makes this radically different approach to education the more urgent today is our growing recognition that we

51

now live in a vastly different world, its resources depleted, its waters polluted, its opportunities diminished. And its peoples are wiser about science and politics. Ours is a time in which men walk on the moon, flash instantaneous motion pictures halfway around the world to show families starving or armies fleeing, or listen to news reports on transistor radios about joblessness in Detroit and racial strife in Cape Town. It is a world with awful inequalities in opportunities and wealth, and now almost everyone realizes that. "In that world of abundance," Martin E. Marty and Dean G. Peerman write in *New Theology*, "most are hungry; in that world of affluence most are unsheltered; in that world of technological mastery, few live by promise or share hope; in that world of potency, few have freedom."

The frightening impoverishment of our planet earth is illuminated in the published reports of Dom Helder Camara and other Roman Catholic bishops in North and in South America. They have reminded us that most Americans can no longer afford an average home; that the top 10 percent of our population has as much income as the entire 50 percent at the bottom, indeed that the top 1 percent receives more income than the bottom 20 percent. With bluntness they aver that our basic cause of poverty is the powerlessness of people over their own political and economic institutions, that most Americans are dependent on social organizations over which they have no control, and that joblessness and inflation result from the high concentration of private control of assets, investment, production, and sales. Faced by such injustice, the church cannot keep still, "As soon as a system ceases to insure the common good to the profit of some party involved, the church must not merely condemn

52

such injustice, but dissociate herself from the system of privilege, ready to collaborate with another that is better adapted to the needs of the time, and more just."

Robert Maynard Hutchins has said that civilization is too near the zero hour to waste our time in educating children; we ought instead to replace them at their desks with adults while we yet have time to alter the drift of our world powers. His assertion cannot be dismissed as dramatic rhetoric; essentially he is in concord with Paulo Freire. Under these urgent conditions education must feature *conscientization,* a relatively new term to which we may as well become accustomed. Conscientization is the process of learning to identify social, political, and economic contradictions, and to take action against oppressive elements that foster them. Conscientization infuses educational projects that battle racism, that attack sexism (here we have called its like concept "consciousness raising"), that demand the tools for development. It is conscientization that inspires Black Power, that motivates the World Council of Churches to fund African bands fighting racism, that strengthens the women's liberation movement, that now begins to stiffen the resistance of senior citizens, and so forth. We have only just begun to hear—as, for example, from Rosemary Ruether—about how it speaks to the sociopolitical aspects of our economy.

Our radical educators now are saying that unless our church educational efforts advance to the front of conscientization and champion these causes, then our churches are actually contributing to the injustices of our times. Barbara Ward has pointed over and over to the urgency for Christians to act in accordance with their creeds, to espouse the justice that their faith emphasizes, and to share the goods that many of them have in such great wealth. Without that leap of faith, she believes, we are doomed within only a few years to feel the unrestrained anger of the undeveloped peoples of this "lopsided world."

We Don't Learn to Swim in Libraries

How ironic, then, that our educational systems continue with so many of their time-worn practices of grading and sorting people, of socializing them into a culture whose isolated continuance is challenged (one is reminded of the players who continued their tennis game while the rockets fell on the suburbs of Saigon), of clinging to the educational *status quo*. In these systems, pupils of every age learn passivity; they are instructed by what has come to be known as the banking concept—the teacher deposits personally owned knowledge in the memories of the pupils for subsequent withdrawal. It is rare that such schools think in terms of the future being any different from the present, whether they are church institutions or public, in child education or adult. We cannot escape the impression that it is not only the oppressed people of underdeveloped countries who need liberation but also our own children.

A close examination of our education, indeed, begins to show ever greater similarities to the situation of Third World countries. William B. Kennedy draws this to our attention:

> We are not in fact a middle class society. We are in fact a society of many wage-earners and a very few wealth-owners, and there is almost no mobility between the two groups. Reform of the American way of teaching therefore demands fundamental change in the American structures of power and wealth.

Anything short of that simply means that we continue training our students for their eventual psychic impoverishment. . . . Our task is as formidable as that of the Latin Americans, and not so very different.

Americans have much to learn from the Third World countries and their *avant garde* educators. We can use their knowledge that education is carried out with and not for the learners, that teachers and pupils learn from each other. Education for liberation is seen not as a gift but as an achievement through their mutual processes of participation.

This emphasis reminds us also of John Dewey's philosophy of education, that we learn from active investment of ourselves—in problem-posing and dialogue, in challenge, and in seeking solutions. We learn by doing, we absorb lessons more deeply "where our feet take us than where our minds go." The growing, becoming person learns what he or she does. In an arresting epigram of Freire, we learn to swim in the water, not in a library.

And now our churches are struggling to find their way into the new, emerging educational programs. Our newer curricula encourage self-actualization as Christians. Is that not also a type of liberation? We are pressed to rediscover our mission, to move our Good News of deliverance well beyond our parish boundaries, to participate in the sufferings and the work of the whole world.

For it is in the community that we realize ourselves and begin to understand God's action in history. The community, far more than the reconstructed environment of the classroom, educates us about humanization and the realities of our times. Developed and transformed by our relationships, our faith can be strengthened through true community and real involvement in the world.

Surely it is the church's mission to enter into that arena, to keep reminding all people of God's will to liberate humanity and to conquer sin and oppression. It is the church's educational task to remind that Christ lives, and that God has acted in him to make each person's life abundant. Its failures have only incidentally been those of the church school; its real failures are in faith and mission. That we need a mutuality between teacher and pupil is not to be denied. Nor do we deny that they must be open to the reconciliation God offers them in Christ. What we are stressing is that they require something more, namely, a caring concern for the deliverance of all humanity from exploitation and depravity. This is education for liberation.

Have This Mind in You

In Nairobi in 1975 the fifth assembly of the World Council of Churches convened Christians from throughout the earth to consider how "Jesus Christ frees and unites." For many who attended that event, this theme of liberation is more than simply the current theological fashion. It is a life-and-death issue to persons from deprived and still undeveloped countries.

We have seen enough by now of churchly resistance to change, of the embarrassing disparity of wealth between the privileged few and the oppressed masses, of the fear among the haves and the threat from the have-nots, of the biblical theme of liberation and hope, to know that we cannot escape our obligation of education for liberation.

Before it is too late, we are challenged to consider what it means to obey One who did not consider it worthwhile to seize equality with God, but shared life with the wretched of the earth, humbling himself even to death—and the death he died was the death of a common criminal. But God highly exalted him; before him our knees bow and our tongues confess that Jesus Christ is Lord. (See Philippians 2.)

To take seriously this incarnational theology involves us necessarily in education for liberation.

Problems in Teaching People to Behave: Clarifying Some Values

Moral education is impossible without the habitual vision of greatness.

Alfred North Whitehead

President Teddy Roosevelt, who had a penchant for acidulous humor, once observed that a bum may steal from a freight car but an educated man learns how he can steal the whole railroad. His dour witticism points up one trenchant fact about education, namely, that it can be used in the service of immorality as effectively as in behalf of morality. Education is seldom, if ever, neutral.

Church educators, who have long realized the need for moral education, *i.e.*, the teaching-learning transaction that inculcates ethical decision and action, find themselves engaged currently in a renewed quest for effective means to accomplish this objective. How to educate for moral responsibility is a puzzling enough problem to stimulate multiple answers and considerable debate. The failures in this quest are too numerous to recount. Through the centuries humankind, over and over again, has asked Plato's ancient question about what virtue is, and how it can be attained. Religious doctrine, moral theology, jurisprudence, political science—these and many more studies are tied to attempts to inculcate morality in humanity.

Our public educational systems were founded upon an expectation that their goal was to teach morality as well as citizenship. The founding fathers, spurred by no end of

58

eighteenth-century idealists like Thomas Jefferson, were convinced that once education became universal our social problems would be solved. The founding fathers believed in the Christian, or at any rate a deist, God and in basic ethical norms of justice, liberty, and charity deriving from the divine order. For them education was to inculcate these values. Indeed, only in recent times has education had any other basis than morality.

But our era can hardly be cited as proof that moral education has succeeded. We witness wholesale public immorality; governments lie to their citizens, corporations conspire to defeat ecology, corrosion accumulates in society. Despite Reinhold Niebuhr's contention that we are moral persons in an immoral society, private morality is actually little better; for here we witness rip-offs by shoplifters, sexual promiscuity, and a nearly contagious denial that we have any responsibility for one another. It is said that an ancient Chinese curse was "May you live in interesting times!" We do; and the average of moral standards is regrettably low in these, our times of interest.

Meanwhile there are mounting cries for reform and for better teaching of morals, a hardly unexpected concomitant of such times. Sharpened demands for distributive justice, some of which are described in chapter 3, accompany a decline in moral obligation. This apparent paradox is explained by Robert Bellah as the result of individual freedom ("Do your own thing"). If our long-held belief is true that a sturdy, secure society rests upon moral understanding of what is right and wrong, good and bad, ethical and unethical, then we are certainly in crisis.

That the churches have failed in their moral education efforts is apparent from considerable data. Both in individual morality and in the social ethic, church teaching, no matter how conscientious, is weighed in the balance and found wanting. Serious Christian educators are everywhere asking how this failure can be reversed and what can be done to correct our virtual neglect of moral education in past years. The answer cannot be simple (e.g., Why, just increase the amount of moral teaching!), for our fault lies not in omitting the subject but in presenting it so poorly. Often we have reminded persons of their duty; but we have done so moralistically, i.e., we have tended to put emphasis on the basis of tithing mint, anise, and cumin and similar picayune points. Or we have taught morality to people through least effective methods, e.g., lecturing them about their ethics. But the moral breakup of our day requires far better means than either of these. Our task here is to examine the data and the means available to church educators.

After a brief survey of the research data concerning moral choices that persons make, we shall review the cognitive-developmental approach to moral education, then examine several viable models that are consistent with the Christian calling.

Evidences of Immoral Choices

Social psychologists have assembled data from a spate of experiments that disillusion us about morality in the private sector. From the many available, we choose two.

Hugh Hartshorne, my one-time teacher in psychology of religion, together with Herbert May, tested school children in a famous set-up test to learn about cheating. It was so arranged that dishonest behavior would be immediately exposed. (Most such psychological experiments are supplied with one-way mirrors through which observers watch, or special papers that reveal changed answers, or other means of checking.) Hartshorne and May concluded that moderate cheating must be the norm. They found that no one was consistently honest or dishonest, but that everyone's behavior varied according to the risk involved or the effort required or the example of their peers.

More recently, Stanley Milgram and his confederates at Yale devised a different type of experiment in which they informed volunteers that the objective was to study the effects of punishment on learning. (The secret objective was actually to discover how far the volunteers would go in deliberately hurting helpless persons.) So-called learners (but actually confederates of the experimenter) were strapped into chairs with unconnected electric wires leading to their flesh. Each time they gave a wrong answer to a question, the volunteer was instructed to press a button and shock the "learner," who, in turn, would yell with apparent pain. Sixty-five percent of the volunteers actually obeyed this order to apply electric shock to a complete stranger who had failed to respond with the approved answer. Since that time this has come to be known as the Eichmann Experiment because the shockers so often explained their behavior by saying that they were only following orders.

Having research on the conditions that lead people into dishonesty and cruelty, it would be helpful if we also had other research available on how positive morality can be developed. Fortunately, just such research is available.

The Cognitive-Developmental Approach to Morality

It is to Jean Piaget we first turn, as practically everyone does, to seek guidance about how the young child develops

61

a sense of morality, or an ability in language or in thinking. Piaget, now an elderly and distinguished scientist, continues to work away in his psychology laboratory and at his writing at the University of Geneva. Through years of painstaking research he has found a way through the puzzle of how the child learns to reason and to arrive at knowledge. Because this inquiry searches out thought processes in the acquisition of knowledge, it is labeled cognitive; because it takes the child through years of growth, it is developmental: hence "the cognitive-developmental approach." Piaget believes this approach to be basic to how the child arrives at his or her concepts of good and evil in an appreciation of moral judgment.

Piaget, after conducting a series of psychological experiments, has reached the conclusion that the developing child moves from an early and rigid position of obedience (because adults are bigger and punitive) later to a more independent position of internalizing his or her own rules. The former position is *heteronomous* (rules from others), the latter *autonomous* (one's own digested rules).

One method of testing this theory is to tell a story and then to query children about how they understand its moral elements. For example, Piaget relates a story of a boy named Henry who climbs up some cupboard shelves to reach forbidden jam and, in doing so, dislodges and breaks a china cup. Children, upon hearing this case narrative, are then asked evaluative questions to test whether they pay more attention to Henry's motive or to the material results connected with this unfortunate accident. Up to age ten, children evidence two clear-cut stages of moral judgment. In the first, they exhibit an *objective responsibility*, that is, they are impressed by the damage done rather than by Henry's intention in snatching at the jam. In the second, called *subjective responsibility,* they note the intention Henry had and they tend to ignore the element of material damage, *i.e.,* the broken cup. This latter tendency to emphasize the intentional aspect, namely, what Henry had in mind as his goal, increases with the children's age. They are moving toward an autonomous moral judgment.

Along with this development of a moral critique, the child is forming his or her conscience. This progresses through three steps: first, blind obedience to authority; second, a recognition of standards of right and wrong; and third, an incorporation of these into one's own sense of guilt. Coincidental to this developing conscience, children begin also to understand a concept of justice, a process that takes them from moral realism (*e.g.,* an absolute position in which it is always wrong to lie) to moral relativism (*e.g.,* some white lies are of value). Now that the child has reached more autonomous moral thinking, she or he will differentiate among those numerous rules that regard other persons with concern, that involve self-respect, and so forth. On the way now to self-discipline, a truly autonomous stance, the child becomes able to avoid the whims of mere self-gratification. Maturity cannot be far off.

Lawrence Kohlberg, a famed psychologist on the faculty of Harvard University, also uses a cognitive-developmental approach to the subject of moral education. He has built upon the foundation of Piaget's earlier work, but with a more sophisticated design involving six developmental stages, an elaborate scoring and measurement system to code interview responses, and a careful theoretical construct.

Like Piaget, Kohlberg also uses a case-study method, telling an open-ended morality tale and then questioning persons about it. Typical of this method is the story of Heinz, whose wife is critically ill from cancer. Heinz learns a local druggist has discovered a new drug that may save his wife; it cost the druggist $200, but for a small dose he now charges $2,000. The frantic husband tries to raise the money but can only borrow about $1,000; so he begs the druggist to sell it more cheaply or to allow deferred payments. The druggist coldly responds, "No, I discovered the drug, and I'm going to make money from it." So the desperate husband breaks into the store to steal the drug for his wife.

The questions then follow: Should the husband have done it—was it right or wrong? Do you believe that your choice that the act is right (or wrong) is a choice that is objectively and universally right, or is it just your personal moral opinion? On the basis of the answers, taken from discussion and interview, Kohlberg and his associates code and record moral positions along a six-stage scale.

Kohlberg's six stages take us through the maturation of ethical reasoning. From the most primitive (a heteronomous level) to the most mature, they are as follows (the nicknames below are not always in the language of Kohlberg):

Pre-conventional level

Stage I. "He's bigger than I am." A stage of physical punishment for wrongdoing; so don't get caught. An obedience-and-punishment orientation.

Stage II. "You scratch my book, and I'll scratch yours." A stage of reciprocity in instrumental hedonism, planned to satisfy one's own needs and occasionally the needs of others. Naïvely egoistic orientation.

Conventional level

Stage III. "You're a good man, Charlie Brown." A stage where moral understanding is based on gaining approval. Behavior is gauged by intention. "He means well" is interpreted as being nice.

Stage IV. "Law and order." A stage of tooth-for-tooth justice that appeals to the rule-bound conformist. Respect for authority and fixed rules of order characterizes him. Not useful for many moral questions. Authority orientation.

Post-Conventional level

Stage V. "Nice neighborhood." A stage wherein we can work our agreements on facts and then lead on to decisions. A legal viewpoint is emphasized, but with the possibility of changing rules in time; the U.S. Constitution fits this description. A social-contract basis of orientation.

Stage VI. "Peak morality." An abstract stage that involves internalized moral principles of justice. The top level where *agape* figures in as a universal ethical principle of justice with a profound respect for persons. Conscience orientation.

Kohlberg argues that these six stages are universal stages of moral development, invariably found in such order from the first to sixth. The moral educator's task is to stimulate upward movement from one stage to another. Cognitive conflict and stories concerning ethical problems are employed to stretch the learner's thinking and deciding.

Kohlberg's disciples (and he has many) claim a variety of advantages for this system of these six ranks of moral reasoning. They hold it is universally applicable and that its schema has been measured cross-culturally with children in various situations. The stages have been empirically tested, and they have held. The unique claim for this construct is that students tend to prefer the highest level they can understand, regardless of the teacher's authority or position. A certain upward mobility seems built into the levels, encouraging students to move to higher levels of ethical judgment.

The six graduated levels appear to avoid one of the weaknesses of much moral reasoning, namely, relativism. Everyone tends to carry around a bag of virtues, Kohlberg contends. Aristotle espoused such virtues as temperance, truth, and justice. Boy Scouts are brave, clean, reverent, and much else. The French Revolutionist displayed liberty, equality, fraternity, and so on. These six moral stages, however, are based on universal principles, the Kohlberg team claims, thus avoiding the inference that everyone carries a different bag of virtues, each relatively as good as another.

In practice, moral judgment can be inculcated by use of these stages through a system of interaction and discussion. This method has been tried in churches and synagogues by the Kohlberg team of researchers, and their claim for it is that it is eminently workable. Their scheme is to arouse moral conflict in discussion and to witness the struggle as a given child begins to push into the next higher stage where some peers are already operating. Gradually they test the thinking of the new stage (they may be moving from stage three's goodness-for-approval's sake to the harder standards of stage four's retributive justice), and they find they prefer it to their previous level. This tentative testing of a new stage is a kind of role-taking, if we may here use George Herbert Mead's concept of trying on a different person's position. It enables one to understand others' moral standards whether one comes to adopt them or not.

But Kohlberg's system is not to be considered replete with advantages. It is also open to several criticisms. I shall cite five. First, although the data can be standardized and measured to record what moral judgments are being learned, the elaborate and complicated scoring system is awkward to utilize and to explain. To the critical observer it appears excessively recondite. Second, the connection between the cognitive aspects and moral aspects of learning is conceded by everyone to be important, and no one wishes to confute Kohlberg's contention that it is; but it remains difficult to demonstrate what that connection is and how to prove that it even exists.

Third, the system is in no way religiously specific, and thus it tends to leave theologically minded persons uneasy about where or whether it fits into church education. That it is adaptable to religious institutions is undoubted, and Kohlberg's avoidance of moral relativism is especially compatible to the thinking of many theologians. But for the present it remains an external plan brought into church education where its fit is loose. Fourth, there appears to be a wide gap between moral judgment and moral actions in this work. To be able to make a cognitive moral decision is not the same as engaging in moral action. It is feasible, in fact, to come to a sophisticated moral judgment without ever taking the next steps toward action at all. To know the good is not necessarily to do the good, no matter what Socrates opined about it. Fifth, the research methods and results that Kohlberg publishes are not always replicated with compatible results by other researchers. Some, indeed (*e.g.,* John H. Krahn), have reached quite different findings that are opposed to his.

Criticisms notwithstanding, the Kohlberg cognitive-developmental studies in moral education are among the most advanced and influential we have; and he levels some of these criticisms at his own work, being a scientist and seeking corrections continuously.

Piaget and Kohlberg then help us to understand the formation of moral judgment, and perhaps that should be enough for us. But it isn't. Another question remains: How do we program moral education, *i.e.,* the planned learning experience, to understand what individual and social morality can be? Indeed, how do we judge these moralities and put them into practice?

How Morality Is Taught and Practiced

The case-study method, used by both Jean Piaget and Lawrence Kohlberg, is one means of teaching the curriculum of moral education. Other methods also include values clarification, discussion and decision-making, simulation games, the supportive fellowship group, and even the hard sell of direct indoctrination.

Case studies and narratives of various forms constitute a favorite choice of moral educators. The relating of morality stories can open up contemporary issues of relevance to students on such topics as ecology, sexuality, world order, racial relations. It is a natural way of using biblical material, and it can take advantage of what Theodore Wedel once called "story theology." One of Kohlberg's associates, Doug Sholl, in fact, has isolated passages from the book of

Genesis to illustrate his method. We see in the story of Lot's choice from the most desirable land from Abram's holdings (Genesis 13) evidence of stage three morality—Charlie-Brown orientation to approval. In the near-sacrifice of Isaac (Genesis 22) we find stage four, law-and-order morality, a maintenance of social order and authority. The advantages of a case-story method are obvious: it exposes the learners to hypothetical dilemmas that can then be argued, making them aware of questions they already have. In such debate they can then take sides, assume roles, establish or exchange positions. As a teaching method it is superior to rote learning and indoctrination through clichés.

Values clarification, a somewhat different approach, invariably is associated with its most famous proponent, Sidney Simon. Essentially a Socratic discussion method as he uses it, its objective is to aid persons to weigh their own set of values. Through this experience they come to clarify their alternatives and begin to connect the cause-and-effect relations in their decision-making.

Simon isolates three levels of education: facts, concepts, and values. He once illustrated how these can be used in a typical church-school lesson on St. Francis. On the *fact level* he asks such questions as: What kind of clothes did St. Francis wear and what did they represent? On the *concept level* he bears in more deeply with questions of which this is typical: How far apart were the lives of the poor and the rich in the early thirteenth century when St. Francis lived? But on the *values level* he asks: How near do the poor live to you? How much concern should you have about their poverty? Have you ever done anything about it?

Values clarifications can be facilitated also by means of diary-keeping, autobiographical writing, reaction sheets, and numerous other methods. The heart of the plan remains in the use of the ever-deepening thrust of questions. And the limitation for church educators is its relativism. It searches out what values we bring, and clarifies which positions we ourselves hold in our pluralistic society. But it has no universal principles. It is less oriented to moving us into higher levels of moral judgment than is Kohlberg's system. That the two could be combined effectively in moral education seems obvious. This is a problem that needs some additional research.

The discussion method hardly constitutes a category by itself, as it is also used along with other ways of moral education. Yet it has been lifted to a special emphasis in the moral education writings of John Wilson, director of the Farmington Trust Research Unit in Moral Education at Oxford University. Wilson's numerous books on the subject reiterate that teachers cannot escape responsibility for moral education; they're into it whether they realize this consciously or not. Educators may have different moral views, as Kohlberg reminded us, and different convictions on procedures of how to settle their differences. But they must recognize that there is a methodology of moral education, and there is a basis for morality for everyone. For one person that basis is Jesus; for another, Mao; for still another, *Das Kapital*. We are therefore compelled into "doing morality," which, for Wilson, is not supplying moral answers for someone's questions from authorities but, rather, open discussion with examples, plus participation in moral education.

Wilson abhors what he characterizes as the "moral realism" school that would coerce persons into moral conformity by means of conditioning, drugs, pressure of

70

status, or even terror, because such methods teach nothing. Moral education must be a teaching-learning transaction, he insists. The learner who participates in rules-making becomes part of a contract. That learner can then rationally accept the regulations because he or she played a major part in its formulation.

Wilson also advocates experimentation with survival situations, *e.g.*, a reconstruction of Golding's *Lord of the Flies,* to give students practice in how to establish moral standards under extreme conditions. Such experimental programs are feasible for church education too, as are other more concentrated experiences. These include camping, weekend retreats, family clusters, simulation games, and conferences, which, because they make possible longer units of continuous time, offer unusual opportunities for practice and interchange. We need such praxis to understand how morality is tested and practiced. Regardless of the circumstances in which the topic of morality is introduced, in the end it will require both example and practice if it is, indeed, to be usable. It still remains true that our learners need less to hear the Christian ethic described than to see it lived.

The Christian's Morality as Calling

The churches have been less than diligent about their moral education during these recent years. Neglecting instruction about individual ethical obligations, they have sometimes added to the problem of moral *malaise* instead of contributing to its solution. Our challenge is to move beyond the cognitive discipline of value judgment, beyond even the affective component with its emphasis upon trust and security. Our challenge is to test our knowledge and judgment of morality by theological ethics. This is not to say—not at all—that we are to eschew the psychological experiments of a Kohlberg or the educational theories of a Wilson as we research our theology. Indeed, quite the contrary: we plan to use the knowledge and wisdom of any discipline to assist us in this very difficult problem. Theology, however, is the picture window through which we look at the data from psychology, anthropology, sociology, and other learning disciplines.

To adopt such a comprehensive view of theological ethics, we must correct some of the unfortunate effects of our church history. Too often in the past, church moralists have interpreted right conduct in terms of restraint and law. But restraining persons from evil acts is a crude measure compared to training them in moral education to be autonomous and responsible. Such restraints do not make people choose to do good: neither handcuffs, time clocks, solitary confinement, chastity belts, guards, nor even teachers. They may only prevent persons from accomplishing undesirable acts. There is a profound difference between the two. Neither does the hard sell in massive pressure by the church to conform to moral laws constitute quality moral education.

To bind Christians by rules and regulations is unworthy of our tradition. It was from such legalism Christ came to set us free. Gerald Slusser has noted:

Certainly no one wishes to counsel disobedience of the commandments, but neither is slavish obedience an appropriate stance for the Christian. The heart of Jesus' battle with the religious leaders of his day lay just here. The Pharisees were the good moral men of their day, yet it was the Pharisees who could never really understand Jesus because he seemed to them to be a lawbreaker, an immoral man. The already given law, like the mores of the social community, may become a basis for irresponsibility. Further, moral obedience can lead to the most flagrant sort of self-righteousness.

For the Christian, morality is not so much rules as it is a calling from God. It is to God we first turn to understand our ethics, for our ethical standards are derived from our theology. In terms of Micah 6:8, our understanding of God's calling precedes our understanding of moral duty: "What does the Lord require of you but to do justice, and to love kindness, and to walk humbly with your God?" The ancient Hebrew, you see, conceived of education as growing in the likeness of God. (The contemporary Greek conceived of education as more of an intellectual enterprise leading to virtue, and Christian education has ofttimes combined these two conceptions.) It is what Paul Tillich called our Ultimate Concern that shapes our ethic. Our perception of right conduct is based on a view of the universe that moral understandings make sense. And it is this that produces legitimization for any society that would organize in accord with such understandings of moral choices.

That God-inspired view of our moral education can accomplish, then, three objectives: (1) it can offer us the picture window through whose frame we see the issues of ethics and of methodology; (2) it can free us to replace mere prohibitions with positive principles, a measure Dietrich Bonhoeffer named responsible freedom; and (3) it can shake us loose from the moral relativism that so easily besets us. We urgently need a viable morality that, as William Kay observes, is not enervated by shifting moral standards and the constantly modified mores that we have in our secularized, pluralistic society. To affirm that different persons hold differing and conflicting values about what is good and evil is of only the slightest use in moral education. The Christian educator goes beyond that point into theological inquiry, ethical clarification, and moral judgment, emphasizing the mutual participation of teacher and learner in ethical decisions rather than dictating moralistic rules.

Much of the problem in trying to teach people to behave will remain with us despite the urgency of countering the immorality of our day, despite some new data on how people learn morality, despite the theological convictions from which we work. It will be so for years to come, for this is a stubborn problem that has been with us for centuries and on which our children, and our children's children, will still be working. Our new hope is that we have discovered some keys to begin to unlock the mysteries.

The Real Impossibility
of Christian Education

Since every Christian has become a new creature by rebirth from water and the holy Spirit, so that he may be called what he truly is, a child of God, he is entitled to a Christian education.

Declaration on Christian Education,
Vatican II.

To be blunt, there is something about Christian education that is impossible. Ours is an assignment that simply cannot be completed in the world we know. As we confront learners in church, we see a peculiar people who are not at home here at all. The most obvious mark about us all is that we are pilgrims, nothing but sojourners in this land, on our way to another place which has real foundations, whose maker and builder is God. The Christian educator is acting neither logically nor morally if he attempts to assist persons to adjust to this world *(De terrenae civitatis)*. We are en route on this journey of faith to quite another destination that God has prepared. It is a location so dissimilar to most experience we have here that we can only describe it in the unusual terms of contrast that set it apart from anything we now know—there shall be no night there, no hunger, no thirst, no pain. Most of our vaunted theories about education, with its principles of experiential learning, of readiness, about practice projects, and the like are ultimately inadequate for preparing persons toward that far-off goal. We have long since settled for a system of churchly compromises.

When we stop to consider this temporal, mortal nature of ours, we at once have more insight about the churning restlessness that permeates the educational efforts of the church. Ours are the people described in the classic Letter to Diognetus, for whom "every land was fatherland, and every fatherland foreign." Here we are, all of us, trying to make the vastness of the world our home, and forever doomed to failure. This is man's essential loneliness, a theme appreciated both by poets and by theologians. In *The Grass Harp,* Truman Capote gives it wistful expression: "It may be that there is no place for any of us. Except we know there is somewhere; and if we found it, but lived there only a moment, we could count ourselves blessed." The ancient Israelite, giving voice to what may be the oldest extant profession of faith, affirms something of the restlessness of our hearts when he poetically repeats a fact of his origin: "A wandering Aramean was my father." Thomas Wolfe, in a lyrical, famous passage from *Look Homeward Angel,* gives it yet another utterance:

> Which of us is not forever a stranger and alone? . . . lost among bright stars on this most weary unbright cinder, lost! Remembering speechlessly we seek the great forgotten language, the lost lane-end into heaven, a stone, a leaf, an unfound door. Where? When?

Today man is convinced not only of his lostness but also of his limited worth. Stranger and pilgrim that he is, he is impressed on many sides with how cheaply he is valued: a mere unit in employment—or unemployment, a number in the armed forces, a punch card in the Internal Revenue Service. And now again existentialism has come to the fore and assisted us in uncovering the nothingness, the insignificance, and the futility in man; but it was there all the time. Some months ago *Harper's* magazine offered one whimsical support for this observation in a mock award "to one Elvis Presley, a complete set of the works of John Calvin, bound in brimstone, for reminding us that mankind is born considerably lower than the angels; but that by God's grace, our periodic epidemics of silliness soon pass." The Bible always looks unflinchingly upon the finitude of man, and with no apology traces his rude origin from the very dust of the earth. But the Bible also pictures man as the beneficiary of a divine Love. He is granted that level a little lower than the angels. He is personally and intimately known by his Creator. In its ultimate expression, one finally can turn to anyone, no matter what her or his character or potential, and say with profound truth: "Christ died for you."

Knowledgeable Christian educators, firmly grounded in their biblical theology, are compelled then to come to terms with man-as-he-is: imperfect and imperfectible, wandering sometimes aimlessly, sometimes "tryin' to make Heaven my home." The church educators dare not bend their strength to helping him adjust to an infected world. That is sin. They cannot map a clear route toward the City of God. That calls for omniscience. They do not necessarily dream up ever newer methods to form Christian character. (Heaven knows that this was the Protestant emphasis of the 1920s and 1930s and is militantly promoted by numerous proponents today.) Rather the Christian educator who sees the work as a theological discipline concerned with the whole ministry seeks to make theology relevant to persons so as to open the way to Christian discipleship through the redemptive community.

For God is at work in this world's history and in eternity; and he has chosen to work through his church, through human lives, through events. Christian education, then, has enormous opportunity quite apart from working for adjustment to the here and now or preparation for the sweet by-and-by. Christian education will relate persons to Jesus Christ, and as his disciples they will come to know him and his will for them. Some educational principles useful in introducing such a relationship must now be examined.

Christian Education Must Be Dramatic

Now no one is so naïve as to suppose that when we have honestly defined our function in terms of discipleship that the issue is resolved. Knowing that it is impractical to describe Christian education solely in terms of relating pilgrims to this world because it is their temporary home, and that we are neither wise enough nor good enough to prepare them for the world to come, we have fallen back on the only plausible plan. If we are confused at times about the *what* of Christian education, we need not be confused about the *who*. Though we are unable to determine the wisest course for people in this pilgrimage, we do know whom to follow.

When you see Christian education in this light, where an attitude of discipleship may be more important than a body of information, it can but deemphasize to some extent the expounding of knowledge and dogma. I am aware of the cogent arguments that we must begin with the proclamation of that which is given by God in Christ. I know full well that Christian education has little validity when it is cut simply to the pattern of persons' needs, without due regard to the body of doctrine. But I do not concede that we have in this argument an either-or debate. Surely within the given tradition, within the proclamation of the faith, one finds sturdy emphasis upon the saving relationship between God and his people. It is here, believe me, that Christian education has its work. Yet many who teach in our church schools apparently subscribe to quite another conviction. There is no guarantee, as Emil Brunner has cautioned us, that the stressing of religious doctrines will make devout Christians of persons. Sometimes I think that we American churchmen have been overtrained in the techniques of assembly lines until we almost suppose that by introducing a combination of doctrines at one end of the production system we can turn out a finished Christian at the other. Technology, however useful it may be in the manufacture of Fords, is not applicable to the education of Christian disciples.

To put it baldly, Christian education is too often weighed down by a surfeit of mere talk. We need, of course, the clear exposition of religious ideas, but we need to remind ourselves regularly that "the kingdom of God does not consist in talk but in power" (I Corinthians 4:20). A quality of commitment is necessary that goes far deeper than the sort of catechetical adjustment that gives neat answers to life's major questions. It was Jesuit mystic, J. P. DeCaussade, who phrased this idea so tellingly in his little book *Abandonment to Divine Providence:*

> We may know all the theory of this work, admirably write and speak thereon, and instruct and direct souls; but if our knowledge be only theoretical, then I would say that in comparison with souls which live and act by the order of God and are guided by His divine will, though ignorant of the theory of its operations or its different effects, and unable to speak thereof, we are like a sick physician compared to ordinary persons in perfect health.

79

CHRISTIAN EDUCATION FOR LIBERATION

The fact is our children, our young people, our adults need not so much to hear the Christian life described again as to see it lived! Real Christian education has to be dramatic, not just auditory. Over a doorway in the College of Preachers at Washington Cathedral is printed a motto: "If you do not dramatize the word, they will not get the message." And is this not what God has done in his speaking to mankind? Words he has used, but also mighty acts. He speaks through history, global and personal. He has spoken through lives, indeed climactically (and I do not mean irreverence) through "the divine charade" in which the Word was made flesh. If Emerson is right that our actions speak so loudly that the words we say cannot be heard above them, then it must be that one of these exceeds the other in dramatic impact. I remember seeing an Italian film a few years ago entitled *Rome Eleven O'Clock*. For English-speaking audiences, the movie had been outfitted with the customary subtitles, flashing in phrases at the bottom of the screen while the cast spoke their native tongue. But when, in a rushing climax, a stairway collapsed and sent a hundred screaming people into a welter of broken bodies, pain, and death, the English translations were omitted. When it became climactic, our sense of the action was sharp enough that we needed no translated words. And we never missed them. A scream of pain in Italian is no different from a cry of pain in English.

Unless words are supplemented by other dramatic symbols, they lose their force. Historians attribute Woodrow Wilson's failure to sell the idea of the League of Nations here in America to his inability to dramatize the issues. How very different from a Martin Luther with his hammer and theses in hand, or an Albert Schweitzer working in surgery! Christian education, in order to win disciples, must be dramatized. It is for this reason, rather than just for the fulfillment of some Dewey principles of education, that in late years we have moved into wider programs of laboratory teaching, field trips, observation, work projects, experiments in group process, and the like. There is no curriculum about Christianity so effective as a life that incarnates the idea.

Replacing the Abstruse with the Real

If our Christian education has at times erred on the issue of wordiness, this has not been the only trouble. Christian educators have also shown an inordinate fondness for theological abstractions. It is difficult to imagine anyone ever being converted to a saving relationship in Jesus Christ through a reading of the history of the Council of Nicea. Abstract principles, which have so important a place in speculative theology, are far from the reality-feeling of the ordinary mortal. Dietrich Bonhoeffer has reminded us that God's commandment revealed in Jesus Christ is always concrete speech, always *to* somebody; it is never abstract speech about something or somebody. Look to the prophets. They did not reduce the cutting edge of their message by making it general or abstract. They used symbols, drama, and words that did not compromise the content. Thus they contribute to the tremendous power of the Bible, which has the habit of presenting universal truths concretely in their impact on human lives. Seldom are the Scriptures concerned in an abstract, intellectual way with "How shall we think?" Their intent far more often is "What shall I do?"

James Thurber tells a fable about a weaver who

innocently queried a silkworm spinning its cocoon. "Where do you get that stuff?" And the silkworm, meaning no harm, replied, "Do you want to make something out of it?" Both of them went away insulted, and Thurber moralizes: "A word to the wise is not sufficient if it doesn't make any sense." There are persons we all know who are for one reason or another virtually incapable of abstract thinking. To formulate much of our Christian teaching in abstract terms is to talk right past their ears and to involve them hardly at all. Our biblical example should lead us to better practice than that. The Old Testament bends over backward to be direct and concrete, sometimes offending the fastidious with its heavy anthropomorphism. But this method is not without purpose, for it kept all thought and discussion of God on a personal level from which no one has any escape. A far cry that is from the abstruse jargon of some theoreticians. Let us pick one example (outside our field) from F. C. S. Northrop: "The answer to the basic problem of our time is as follows," he wrote. "The esthetic, intuitive, purely empirically given component in man and nature is related to the theoretically designed and indirectly verified component by the two-termed relation of epistemic correlation."

Such obscuratism is not unknown to the church, where our evangelistic concern for persons should prevent us from such transgressions. Theodore Wedel was quite right in saying that just as we change our twenty-dollar bills into small change before we board the bus, we must also take our theological currency and change it into coinage recognizable by those we hope to teach. To do this we ordinarily call upon analogies in relationships. Jesus used this method so frequently that a host of examples spring to mind: the kingdom of God is like a grain of mustard seed; he compares himself to a door; he makes an epigram from the man who hears the Word, likening him to a man who builds his house on rock foundation. There is no avoiding these analogies, because they are necessary to meaning and communication. You will recall that Thomas Aquinas taught that all language about God must be analogical. But all language about anything is reduced to analogy, for we think in a series of metaphors. Habitually we relate new information to old information, and we explain almost nothing in terms of itself but only in terms of other familiar things.

Another quite familiar way that we work our way out of the impasse to which abstraction leads us is through our personal relationships. There is a language of relationships that teaches profoundly. It is in this realm that the parent operates, and this relationship conditions children in ways that remain with them for life.

How profoundly we educate our children will never be completely plumbed. Our affection, our handling of problems, our humor are all parts of a living heritage that our children carry with them to fashion their own mores and to lift their own spirits. We once naïvely assumed that children could be made socially and morally responsible by teaching them concepts of right and wrong and by making personal demands upon them for achievement. We now know, as Luther Woodward says, "that children learn to discipline their own impulses and to set acceptable moral and social goals for themselves in the concrete rather than in the abstract. They grow up morally and socially by having a pleasant, satisfying experience with someone whom they love and trust, in short, by hero worship, the 'hero' being most commonly the father or mother.''

Martin Buber has referred to this relationship as education in dialogue—the children know that they are unceasingly addressed in a dialogue of love that never breaks off. ''In the face of the lonely night which threatens to invade, they lie preserved and guarded, invulnerable, clad in the silver mail of trust.''

The Receptivity Factor

The high importance of our relationships in teaching becomes apparent when we think of the attitude of the learner himself. Nothing is ever taught until someone has learned, we are assured. Which is to say that the best intentioned teacher in the world may get nowhere unless there is some preparation on the part of the learner, some climate of expectation there. *Quid quid recipitur, ad modum recipientis recipitur:* anything that is received is received according to the mood and capacity of the receiver. Gordon Jackson, in *Religious Education,* points out that a religious statement—*e.g.,* Jesus Christ died on a cross—is devoid of meaning to one whose experience has not conditioned him to understand it. In addition to that problem is a related one—two persons often receive the identical information in strikingly variant ways. Because of their past, their relationships, their subjective understanding, and their conditioning, their hearing may be affected as unhappily as in the case of the weaver and the silkworm. Christian tradition has always been subject to this same risk, and historians can point to numerous times when the message was muted or added to or diluted. For this danger the

Christian educator must ever be on watch. (And the alternative methods of teaching I have suggested—teaching through relationships, analogies, or drama—are at least as open to this abuse as oral tradition and the unwritten word.)

Ironical though it is, a schoolboy can learn in one hour a body of fact that took centuries for mankind to discover. As Alan Paton says, "In a minute I am told a secret that a man has struggled a lifetime to wrest from the unknown." But this observation has scant transfer to Christian education. Here it is possible for one to be told the facts of the faith of centuries without in the least understanding what they have to do with one's personal life and choice. Unless the saving truth is internalized, Christian education has not really taken place.

When the Scriptures are communicated in true Christian education, they are read just this way. They are studied not for their own sake (which approaches bibliolatry), but that revelation of truth and life might come through them. They are studied not to assemble a host of facts to help one in quiz program competition, but to point the direction to a saving relationship in Christ. The late David Roberts was quite apt in saying, "Acceptance of doctrine can be vital only when it is an attempt to formulate in words and concepts something which actually happens in the life of man."

And this is the breakthrough in Christian education. It is at that point where the learner identifies the Word as relevant to himself. There is no other experience like it. There was Augustine in his garden, torn by guilt and conflict within, when he heard the voice of a neighboring child singing, *"Tolle et lege"* ("Take and read"). And that voice led him to pick up Paul's Letter to the Romans, where he found himself reading, "Not in reveling and drunken-

85

ness, not in debauchery and licentiousness, not in quarreling and jealousy. But put on the Lord Jesus Christ, and make no provision for the flesh, to gratify its desires.'' This proved to be the mystical experience that brought peace and real conversion to Augustine—his breakthrough. Or centuries later there was Martin Luther wrestling with Scripture, trying to make sense out of another section of this same Letter to the Romans. Then one day it all came clear. ''The just shall live by his faith'' broke through to him as a message of mercy and grace, so that later he was to profess, ''This passage of Paul became to me a gate to heaven.'' Has it ever been that way with you? Did you find old truths breaking through to you in some new way because now you were ready to receive them? It could come in a time of study. It could arrive in a Calvary experience of suffering. It might overcome you at a time of heartfelt gratitude. Then you begin to see aspects you had somehow previously overlooked, and you begin to see that God is actually the great ''I Am'' rather than the great ''He Was,'' as Rufus Jones used to say. Thus caught up in the contemporaneity of the faith, you begin anew to know what it means to say, ''While we were yet sinners Christ died for us'' (Romans 5:8).

But with God All Things Are Possible

If then you wish to ask me what is the difference between the goals of Christian education as I define it and the purposes of Christian evangelism, I can only reply that I see no difference. Functionally these may be defined in different ways, and in practice we have known all too often of each being carried on in some manner without reference to the other. But ideally Christian education should always be evangelizing; evangelism ought ever to be educational. *Traducere est evangelizere:* to teach is to evangelize. Indeed the whole church is involved in this work; and the sooner they all realize it, the better will be the quality of our teaching. Heaven knows that the church ought to be doing the finest job in education anywhere instead of tolerating a pale imitation of public-school standards but without system and without zeal.

Let us know it once and for all: the whole church educates! The preacher in his pulpit as surely as the teacher in a class; the every-member canvasser and the usher on the side aisle, the choir in rehearsal and the scout troop on a hike—all these are educational situations, and in them wittingly or unwittingly we are constantly teaching for good or for ill. James D. Smart, in his book *The Teaching Ministry of the Church,* tells of the West Coast church that found itself in the midst of anti-Nisei and anti-Japanese discrimination. About the many injustices in that community the pastor kept a discreet silence, for he recognized that any outcry could cripple a forthcoming financial drive for their new building. Well, he gained the new church building, "but he and his congregation created a context for education in which no pupil could rightly understand a prophet of the Old Testament or Jesus Christ in the New without damning that church!"

Yet the churches have often applied brakes when the educational enterprise begins to roll. They see Christian character as a fine thing but may conclude that this matter of Christian discipleship carries a good thing too far for most people—indeed for some clergy. The ideal of absolute devotion, an ideal that is expected to be the mark of those who are called into the redemptive community, is so rare that when we find it we rejoice exceedingly and call attention to that church excessively. Yet here and there we find a fellowship who acknowledge themselves as pilgrims, strangers in the here and now, but they know their Lord and hence are better aware of themselves as redeemed sinners.

Our main difficulty has been that as educators we have been only humanists, somehow supposing that all the plans and schedules and administration and curricula depended upon us alone. But Christian education, in common with every other endeavor of the church, awaits Pentecost. And Pentecost will come as surely as God in Christ is ever reaching out to his children to seek, to forgive, and to save. And when that power descends upon us to flame in some new cloven form we shall acknowledge that we alone were all but helpless to bring it about. But then we shall appreciate anew that with God all things are possible.

Why the Conspiracy of Silence About Eschatology in Church Education?

When God, in the supreme moment of teaching
came into this world in Jesus of Nazareth, he came
with no neutrality. In Christ, God took sides,
once and for all, in the final and ultimate terms.

Stephen F. Bayne, Jr.

Something akin to a conspiracy of silence exists among major Protestant denominations in the manner they all but ignore teachings about eschatology, the doctrine of last things. It almost amounts to a tacit agreement to allow the independent curriculum publishers to handle this subject (sometimes with excessive attention). Yet the Bible has inalienable convictions about the eschaton built into its very structure. Norman F. Langford, in a brilliant paper, has described the New Testament as "unambiguously eschatological"; and Emil Brunner observes that "from A to Z (the Old Testament) is eschatological, directed towards a goal which God gives his people." Moreover the traditional lectionaries contain a score or more of eschatological lections to be read in worship annually, while catechisms and the ancient creeds abound in eschatological references. How is it then that a theme so central to the biblical message and so prominent in the lectionary receives such short shrift in wide areas of church education? There are, I believe, four outstanding causes for this curious situation.

CHRISTIAN EDUCATION FOR LIBERATION

Imagery of the Second Coming

The imagery of the Second Coming of Christ and a final judgment has become esthetically objectionable, morally unacceptable, or scientifically ludicrous to vast numbers of our people. We are embarrassed by literal interpretations of these eschatological passages, by paintings that depict the sufferings of the damned, by stories that lay stress on the terrors of lost souls. Theologians are at pains to get over the symbolism of eschatology quickly and to get on to its significance. Thus Karl Barth insists that these are metaphors of ultimate reality and that we must repress our images of judgment as an event. John Baillie explains these references as myths of judgment that really mean for us the resolution of conflict. Emil Brunner reminds us that we have no real picture at all of the final cosmos. Reinhold Niebuhr places the matter in historical context, noting that we probably have to take symbols seriously in order to understand history aright; thus "the symbol of the second coming can neither be taken literally nor dismissed as unimportant." And Alan Richardson drily observes that we can hardly count on Oriental myths to calculate with accuracy the schedule of the eschaton.

The very idea of Jesus becoming a stern judge is unthinkable to a pedagogical tradition that has projected an image of the tender, loving Nazarene as a friend to little children and brother to all mankind. Church school lessons for kindergarten and primary departments are replete with references to a considerate, gentlemanly Master. It is seemingly too harsh, even years later, to teach about a Jesus who turns out to be stern just where we had expected him to be tender, or demanding in instances where we had hoped he would be sympathetic. That John Calvin was troubled by this same quandary is seen in his rumination from *Institutes:*

> It is a source of peculiar consolation that he will preside at the judgment . . . for how could a most merciful Prince destroy his own people? How could a head scatter his own members? . . . Indeed, it is no inconsiderable security that we shall stand before no other tribunal than that of our Redeemer from whom we are to expect our salvation.

Karl Barth, also seeking to place a more positive face upon this matter, draws our attention to the principle that judgment resolves conflict, and that in the Bible a judge is not one who rewards some and punishes others but one who creates order and restores what has been destroyed.

It is not to be wondered that church educators who look to biblical theologians for their aegis become confused and leave the promulgation of a Second Coming to the Russellites, the Millerites, and the Seventh Day Adventists. Until they have some clearer guidance on how to relate thought categories of the Bible to our day so that they can show their contemporaneity, they are likely to allegorize to demythologize, to moralize, and (especially) to ignore.

Church Educators Believe in Secular Progress

Church educators are too imbued with a secular belief in progress to find much place for a doctrine that speaks of calamity and utter finality. The marked influence of progressive education upon the Sunday church school can be seen in dozens of ways. Interest in play therapy, demonstration teaching, experiment, workshops, and discussion methods are but a few of the pieces of apparatus from this movement. Many of these have enriched denominational curricula, but with them was imported a pervading optimism about humanity and expectation of inevitable progress that has been more harmonious with the liberal movement than with biblical scholarship. Proponents of progressive education have had a propensity toward a tomorrow-will-be-better philosophy; and, as the modern church school has looked to public education for much of its inspiration, this rosy expectation has often been uncritically appropriated.

Progressive education, in the words of one of its most articulate apologists, Theodore Brameld, "offers a new world view provided, not by speculation by metaphysics, but by the sciences of man." Man, in his turn, does not find it convenient to contemplate either his own mortality or an end to his world. Stubbornly he maintains his will to live, and his mind cannot tolerate a continuing reminder of his finality. We have learned that our time is not really tense about nuclear warfare because we seldom think enough about it to be frightened by its threat; so we should not be surprised that the constant expectation of the eschaton eventually relaxed its hold on first-century Christians too.

Nevertheless, Christian faith is not without its own confidence in progress. Oddly enough, such progressive leanings are not isolated from a doctrine of eschatology but are intimately connected to it. The vast difference between Christian progress and the progressive education of secular progress is to be found in their basic assumptions. One places its bet on evolutionary advances brought about by reconstructionist possibilities in man. The other puts its hope in God. The grim prophecies of Matthew 24 are a part of the eschatological story, but so is the earnest expectation that the end to this cosmos involves God's coming creation in renewal and completion of that which is now imperfect. The Scriptures lead us to hope even in the midst of tribulation. They help us to see that, in spite of earthbound calamities, our citizenship is in heaven, and that the tension between fear of the eschaton and hope in God that characterized first-century Christianity is also with us today.

Our hope, too, is rooted in Christ. We also must be able to understand what God is saying to us in current history through wars and rumors of wars, through plagues and hurricanes, death and destruction. His message for our time is relevant not only to the child in a fifth-grade class but also to the man dying of heart disease. Our hope is held out to one who sees the end close at hand as well as to another who may see *chronos* in short, successive steps. It has to be that way. Samuel Johnson once chided a preacher for planning a series of sermons for prisoners in the Tower of London, bcecause a number of his hearers expected to be hanged before the series could be completed. Yet this is the way of life. The eschaton has a personal dimension. Of two women grinding in the mill, one will be taken and the other left. Of two men working in the field, one will be taken and the other left. There is no inevitable progress guaranteed for everyone in this world: "Onward, Upward, Outward" is a deceptive slogan. Ours is a time that could be interrupted at any moment, and this is a truth that the world may now understand better than the church! Educators are reminded of the gruesome facts of impending destruction by candid words from Harrison Brown, Hannah Arendt, Norman Cousins, and a host of others. It just may be that now, when secular educators tend less often to believe so blithely in inevitable progress, the Christian educator could turn to

93

them and show them who is our true ground for hope. It is a lesson we also need to turn inward toward the churches.

Eschaton Is Beyond Educators' Control

The eschaton is completely beyond the ability of men, even the educators, to affect or to control. Education, both within the church and without, has a strong bent toward the manipulation of environment. Lesson preparation, influencing the climate of learning, or planning a curriculum are part of this process. Education of every kind emphasizes discipline, organization, and measurable attainment. In each of these areas the educator attempts to maintain enough control to ensure that objectives are reached without placing free persons under duress. So he works with grading, testing, and peer-group classifications. Not unnaturally, the church educator picks up much of this apparatus and transfers it, sometimes uncritically, into the parish. It cannot be doubted that much of this transfer has been of value, embuing a rather haphazard pedagogical procedure with some form and order. Nevertheless, with the apparatus has come, as one could have expected, some of the presuppositions of secular education. And one such presupposition is that if we can correctly analyze the readiness of the pupil for learning, we can then lead him to the change that has been set as the objective of the course. The church, therefore, sees no end of character research, motivational testing, developmental theory, educational goals, self-rating scales, evaluation sessions, and so forth.

Imagine, then, the resistance of some religious educators to a concept of the divine initiative. It cannot be truly said that they doubt the power of God to change lives and instead trust their own abilities more. But it can be said that their actions make it appear that such is their position.

Developmental concepts of learning have contributed much to religious education. For this we can only be grateful. The contributions, however, have also included an understanding that change takes place through a series of developments in the life of a person that advances from infancy to maturity. But the Christian concept of redemption is not the same thing as developmental education. Redemption is the making of a new creature out of a person, becoming something entirely new and remade. This is not limited to gradual development but can also be a drastically sudden changeover in conversion. The new creation is not simply a somewhat more developed person but an utterly different one. So radical a transformation may not be possible for graded education at all, but may be suited only to a more miraculous climax. Even though the church educator and his secular counterpart have shared insights and techniques up to this point, it is here that they might part company. A biblically grounded Christian educator knows how limited is his ability and how dependent he is upon the prevenient grace of God when it comes to making a new creation. As long as the end of education is improvement, we seem to know our way. When the end of education is redemption, we realize that the labor is not wholly within our hands.

Eschatology faces the reluctant church educator with a reminder that none of us moves toward God so much as he comes toward us. He does not wait for us to inch our way to him, but invites us, leads us, falls into step with us. This encounter is not something that clever men have thought up, but a leading of the Spirit. His is the divine initiative. As

Karl Barth points up: "This goal of hope does not stand somewhere and we must laboriously build the road to it, but . . . it says in the Confession, *Venturus est*. Not that we must come; it is He who comes" The feverish busywork of so much church education is shown up for its shallowness and for its fallacious presupposition, namely, that it all depends upon our own human effort. The *via lucis* toward new creaturehood necessitates divine guidance (and faith in that guidance) before we and those we teach ever become new creations. "It does not yet appear what we shall be, but we know that when he appears we shall be like him" (I John 3:2).

Church Education Goals Here and Now

Church education tends to assume that its goals are so earthbound that we seem limited to teaching persons for here and now. The conviction that Christians are strangers and pilgrims on the earth, en route to a city whose maker and builder is God, is too seldom emphasized in church school publications. If our citizenship is elsewhere, as the New Testament holds, that hope is underplayed in denominational curricula. The question might frankly be put: Why should we be educating those whose future is not here? But the Christian hope is equally for the first hour of life and for the last. To answer Dr. Johnson's jibe about preaching a series of sermons to men about to die, this is appropriate and defensible. We shall all die, and the hour of our personal eschaton is unpredictable. Ours indeed may be a dying civilization, and it urgently needs the Word of God.

Christian education dare not avoid the nearly impossible task of teaching persons both for next things and for last things as well. Perhaps we can never take step-by-step education for granted, even though it is the kind at which we are most adept. But we who are in the world, yet not of it, must work in encompassible units, leaving to God the larger transformation, of which we are incapable. In the time that remains, a time of essential uncertainty, we weep as though we weep not, rejoice as though we rejoice not, and buy as if possessing nothing. As in the days of his flesh, we can sense a foreshortening of time and the urgency of our task. Here again we see how the *didache* can never be divorced from *kerygma*. Unless that which we teach is shot through with the proclamation of the Word and the resounding note of urgency, our teaching is not the whole truth.

The word of already-and-not-yet has to be spoken through our church educational efforts. We must candidly review that our security is less to be found here and now than in him who is to come. We who are so impressed by and so distressed by the fleetness of time must reflect that, for God, time can be of a different nature entirely and that what is future for us could be the eternal present for him. Indeed our message must reckon with the realization that the new age is already upon us and that the Bible reaches us so directly because of its contemporaneity. Difficult though it is, church education must face the challenge of explaining that for us our *kairos* may be here and may be now. And that changes our approach. Under such conviction we would see that to educate for the present alone is a fallacy, for the present and the future are both upon us in realized eschatology. Our time is in his hands.

Next Steps and Ultimate Steps

These four common factors have quite evidently contributed to the widespread neglect of the subject and meaning of

97

eschatology in much of church education. We have noted within the cirticisms some possible correctives, but there are others worthy of mention.

To meet the issue of eschatology is not as otherworldly as the church educator may have supposed. Those who have believed devoutly in the eschaton have not simply folded their hands in pious resignation but have often been the very ones to move into resolute action. Because they so believed, they acted. The early Protestants were certain of God's omnipotence and of their own frailty; but many of them are shown in history to have been industrious, conscientious, and ethical, *e.g.,* the Calvinists with their exaggerated emphasis on predestination. Knowing that they were moving to meet their Lord and, more significantly, that he was coming to meet them, they worked for their daily bread but also for their faith. Christianity can be shown to have been most practical at several periods when it was most eschatological in mood.

The coming of the Lord demands that talents be used constructively, that lamps be lighted, that work be done, and debts be cleared. The Apostle Paul looked to the brief time remaining in the world known to him and therefore stressed the Christian ethic, not carelessness nor apathy. It was because the end was understood to be close, and not in spite of it, that he taught. It is true that he attempted less to sway the culture of the times than he did the persons within the *koinonia*. But when time had passed (no man knows the hour) and the church had become more influential, Christians launched into social ethics and began to speak out on how society should conduct itself. Our educational efforts need not consider eschatology to be incongruous with Christian ethics. Ethics must also face the future life of

WHY THE CONSPIRACY OF SILENCE?

each one of us as well as of our world so greatly in need of redemption.

So church education can look both to next steps and to ultimate steps. We need not sell out to a humanistic assumption that our future is limited to this world. Neither need we turn our backs on the best that is known about learning theory and developmental psychology. These we can utilize without confusion and without a blind optimism about the possible results. Such a difficult combination of doctrines in tension will demand a rethinking of our remnant philosophy; but when we have reviewed our place in the remnant, and when we have humbly acknowledged our position, this should become feasible. In so doing, we need not get hung on the Weiss-Schweitzer horn of nineteenth-century liberalism and a supposition that the eschaton must be interpreted as purely future to a mistaken early church, nor need we be impaled on that other horn, elected by so many of our denominational publishing houses, of ignoring the doctrine of eschatology altogether.

Our way out, I believe, lies not in attempting to resolve the tension at all, but in grasping it. Oscar Cullmann and C. H. Dodd have shown us a clue in interpreting the last days as already having arrived, a victory even now within our grasp, a salvation now assured, and a new creation within our lives, which, by God's grace, is possible even now. We have begun to deal candidly with historical criticism in church-school lessons. There is no reason that we cannot have the same candor in regard to the hard sayings of the New Testament regarding doctrines of ultimate finality. Dying persons in a dying civilization need hope. The paradox is that when we open the lessons of eschatology we are not avalanched by despair, but see that it is shot through

99

with hope of our salvation from the very perils it describes. We can then see that our hope lies not in scientific progress or in education per se, nor in feverish attention to works of merit, but in God who was in Christ reconciling this infected world unto himself. In the midst of our need we shall catch a glimpse of our hope. ''Now when these things begin to take place, look up and raise your heads, because your redemption is drawing near'' (Luke 21:28).

Bibliography

Adams, Henry. *The Education of Henry Adams*. New York: Houghton Mifflin, 1918.

Alves, Rubem A. "Theology and the Liberation of Man." In *New Theology No. 9*, ed. Martin E. Marty and Dean G. Peerman. New York: Macmillan, 1972.

Barth, Karl. *Dogmatics in Outline*. New York: Harper, 1959.

————. *The Epistle to the Romans*. London: Oxford University Press, 1918.

Bayne, Stephen F. "God Is the Teacher." In *The Christian Idea of Education*, ed. Edmund Fuller. New Haven: Yale University Press, 1957.

Bellah, Robert. *The Broken Covenant*. New York: Seabury Press, 1975.

Berger, Peter. *The Sacred Canopy*. Garden City, N.Y.: Doubleday, 1967.

Berne, Eric. *Games People Play*. New York: Grove Press, 1964.

Bonhoeffer, Dietrich. *Ethics*. Ed. Eberhard Bethge. New York: Macmillan, 1955.

————. *Letters and Papers from Prison*. Ed. Eberhard Bethge. New York: Macmillan, 1971.

Bradford, Leland. "The Teaching-Learning Transaction." *Adult Education*, Vol. II, No. 3.

Brameld, Theodore. "A Reconstructionist View of Education." In *Philosophies of Education*, ed. Philip Phenix. New York: Wiley, 1961.

Brightman, Edgar S. *Personality and Religion*. New York: Cokesbury Press, 1934.

Brown, Robert McAfee. *Religion and Violence*. Philadelphia: Westminster Press, 1973.

Bruner, Jerome S. *The Process of Education*. Cambridge: Harvard University Press, 1960.

————. *Toward a Theory of Instruction*. Cambridge: Harvard University Press, 1966.

Brunner, Emil. *The Christian Doctrine of Creation and Redemption*, Dogmatics, Vol II. Philadelphia: Westminster Press, 1952.

————. *The Divine Imperative*. New York: Macmillan, 1942.

Buber, Martin, *Between Man and Man*. New York: Macmillan, 1947.

Bultmann, Rudolf. *Jesus Christ and Mythology*. New York: Scribner's, 1958.

Calvin, John. *Institutes of the Christian Religion, Book II*. 7th American ed. Philadelphia: The Presbyterian Board of Christian Education, 1936.

Camara, Helder, *et al.* "Gospel and Revolution." In *New Theology No. 6,* ed. Martin E. Marty and Dean G. Peerman. New York: Macmillan, 1969.

Cantor, Nathaniel. *The Teaching-Learning Process*. New York: Holt, Rinehart and Winston, 1953.

Case, Shirley Jackson. *Christianity in a Changing World*. New York: Harper, 1941.

Celestin, George. "A Christian Looks at Revolution." In *New Theology, No. 6,* ed. Martin E. Marty and Dean G. Peerman. New York: Macmillan, 1969.

Cyril. *Cyril of Jerusalem and Nemesius of Emesea,* ed. William Telfer. The Library of the Christian Classics, Vol. IV. Philadelphia: Westminster Press, 1955.

DeCaussade, J. P. *Abandonment to Divine Providence*. New York: Benziger Brothers, 1945.

Freire, Paulo. *The Pedagogy of the Oppressed*. New York: Herder and Herder, 1970.

Graham, William Franklin. *America's Hour of Decision*. Wheaton: Van Kampen Press, 1951.

Hamilton, William. *The New Essence of Christianity*. New York: Association Press, 1961.

Hartshorne, Hugh, and May, Herbert. *Studies in the Nature of Character*. New York: Macmillan, 1928.

Herzog, Frederick. "The Isenheim Altarpiece." *The Christian Century,* March 26, 1975.

Highet, Gilbert. *The Art of Teaching*. New York: Alfred A. Knopf, 1950.

Hollander, Edwin P. *Principles and Methods of Social Psychology*. 2nd ed. London: Oxford University Press, 1971.

BIBLIOGRAPHY

Illich, Ivan. *After Deschooling, What?* New York: Harper, 1973.
————. *The Church, Change and Development*. Chicago: The Urban Training Center Press, 1970.

John XXIII, Pope. *Pacem in Terris*. New York: Ridge Press/ Odyssey Press, 1964.

Kay, A. William. *Moral Education*. London: Linnet Brooks, 1975.

Kennedy, William B. "Education for Liberation and Community." *Religious Education*, Vol. LXX, No. 1.

Kohlberg, Lawrence. *Moral Judgment Interview and Procedures for Scoring*. Cambridge: Moral Education and Research Foundation, Harvard University, 1973.
————. "Moral Stages and Sex Education." In *Sexuality and Values*, ed. Mary S. Calderone, M.D. New York: Association Press, 1975.

Koyama, Kosure. *Waterbuffalo Theology*. Maryknoll: Orbis Books, 1974.

Krahn, John H. "A Comparison of Kohlberg's and Piaget's Type I Morality." *Religious Education*, Vol. LXVI, No. 5.

Langford, Norman F. "Eschatology and Christian Education." *Nexus*, February, 1961.

Leonard, George B. *Education and Ecstasy*. New York: Delacorte Press, 1968.

Lochman, J. M. "Ecumenical Theology of Revolution." In *New Theology No. 6*, ed. Martin E. Marty and Dean G. Peerman. New York: Macmillan, 1969.

Lynn, Robert W.; and Wright, Elliott. *The Big Little School*. New York: Harper, 1971.

Macintosh, Douglas Clyde. *Theology as an Empirical Science*. New York: Macmillan, 1927.

McLuhan, Marshall, with Wilfred Watson. *From Cliché to Archetype*. New York: Viking Press, 1970.

Mao Tse-tung. *Quotations from Chairman Mao Tse-tung*. New York: Praeger, 1968.

Marty, Martin E., and Peerman, Dean G. eds. *New Theology No. 6*. New York: Macmillan, 1969.

Marx, Karl. *Capital: A Critique of Political Economy*. Ed. Frederick Engels. New York: International Publishers, 1967.

Maslow, Abraham. *Motivation and Personality*. New York: Harper, 1954.

Maves, Paul. *The Church and Mental Health*. New York: Scribner's, 1953.

Mead, George Herbert. *Mind, Self and Society*. Chicago: University of Chicago Press, 1934.

Mead, Margaret. *Culture and Commitment*. Garden City, N.Y.: Doubleday; Natural History Press, 1970.

Michonneau, Abbé Georges. *Revolution in a City Parish*. Westminster, Md.: Newman Press, 1956.

Milgram, Stanley. *Obedience to Authority*. New York: Harper, 1973.

Moltmann, Jürgen. "Toward a Political Hermeneutics of the Gospel." In *New Theology No. 6*, ed. Martin E. Marty and Dean G. Peerman. New York: Macmillan, 1969.

Niebuhr, Reinhold. *Moral Man and Immoral Society*. New York: Scribner's, 1932.

————. *The Nature and Destiny of Man*, Vol II. New York: Scribner's, 1941–43.

Paton, Alan. "The Person in Community." In *The Christian Idea of Education*, ed. Edmund Fuller. New Haven: Yale University Press, 1957.

Paul VI, Pope. *Populorum Progressio*. New York: The Paulist Press, 1967.

Piaget, Jean, *et al. The Moral Judgment of the Child*. Glencoe: Free Press, 1948.

Rath, Louis E.; Harmin, Merrill, and Simon, Sidney B. *Values and Teaching*. Columbus: C. E. Merrill Books, 1966.

Reber, Robert. *World Development as an Aim of the Church's Educational Work*. Nashville: Division of Education of The United Methodist Church, 1974.

Richardson, Alan. *The Political Christ*. Philadelphia: Westminster Press, 1973.

Rogers, Carl. "The Facilitation of Significant Learning." In *Instruction: Some Contemporary Viewpoints*, ed. Laurence Siegel. San Francisco: Chandler Publishing Co., 1967.

Rokeach, Milton. "Paradoxes of Christian Belief." In *Religion in*

BIBLIOGRAPHY

Transition, ed. Jeffrey K. Hadden. New Brunswick, N.J.: Transaction Books, 1970.

Ruether, Rosemary. *Liberation Theology*. New York: Paulist Press, 1972.

Sayers, Dorothy. *The Mind of the Maker*. London: Methuen, 1941.

Shaull, Richard. "Christian Faith as Scandal in a Technocratic World." In *New Theology No. 6*, ed. Martin E. Marty and Dean G. Peerman. New York: Macmillan, 1969.

Sholl, Doug. "The Contributions of Lawrence Kohlberg to Religious and Moral Education." *Religious Education*, Vol. LXVI, No. 5.

Simon, Sidney B. "Value Education." In *Colloquy on Christian Education*, ed. John H. Westerhoff, III. Philadelphia: United Church Press, 1972. (See also Rath, Louis E., *et al.*)

Skinner, B. F. *The Technology of Teaching*. New York: Appleton-Century-Crofts, 1968.

Slusser, Gerald H. *A Dynamic Approach to Christian Education*. Philadelphia: Westminster Press, 1968.

Smart, James D. *The Teaching Ministry of the Church*. Philadelphia: Westminster Press, 1954.

Tillich, Paul. *The Religious Situation*. New York: Meridian Books, 1956.

Ward, Barbara. *The Angry Seventies*. Rome: The Pontifical Commission Justice and Peace, 1970.

———. *The Lopsided World*. New York: W. W. Norton, 1968.

Wedel, Theodore. *The Christianity of Main Street*. New York: Macmillan, 1950.

Westerhoff, John H., III. *A Colloquy on Christian Education*. Philadelphia: United Church Press, 1972.

———. *Values for Tomorrow's Children*. Philadelphia: Pilgrim Press, 1973.

Whitehead, Alfred North. *The Aims of Education*. New York: Macmillan, 1929.

Wilson, John. *Practical Methods of Moral Education*. London: Heinemann Educational Books, 1972.

———. *A Teacher's Guide to Moral Education*. London: Geoffrey Chapman, 1973.

Woodward, Luther. "Fostering Mental Health Through the Church Program." In *The Church and Mental Health,* ed. Paul B. Maves. New York: Scribner's, 1953.

Wynn, J. C. "Christian Family Living." *The Christian Century,* March 3, 1954.

————. "The Paucity of Eschatology in Church Education." *Religious Education,* Vol. LX, No. 2, p. 106.

————. "Christian Education for Pilgrims." *Religious Education,* Vol. LIV, No. 5, p. 406.

Index

INDEX